THE
CUSTODY LAWYER

Janet McCullar

DEDICATION

For my amazing son, Sammy, in gratitude for all of his
encouragement and support of his working mom.

ACKNOWLEDGMENTS

To Michelle Borquez, a total BOSS, who took an idea, and with the help of Sherrie Clark, made a dream reality.

To my clients who entrusted me with their work, thus helping me grow as a lawyer and a human!

To Jodi and Jennifer, my trusted sidekicks.

DISCLAIMER

This book is not intended to be legal advice about your divorce or custody dispute, nor mental health advice about you, your spouse, partner, or children. This book is for educational purposes only. For legal advice about your divorce, consult a divorce attorney in your area. For mental health advice, contact your local psychological or psychiatric association for help in finding a qualified professional.

INTRODUCTION

During my twenty-five years as an attorney, I have focused mainly on custody work and litigation. I know what works well and what doesn't work at all. I wanted to use my experience to give parents a tool that would not only help them but let them know they're not alone.

Furthermore, I too went through a divorce and was confronted with some of the same questions my clients asked me. Even though my custody experience was amicable, and I'm a custody lawyer, there were still many unknowns from a parent's perspective. I never had to think about things, like what to tell my four-year-old son or how to help him adjust to such a big change. I began to understand the anger, mistrust, sadness, and other emotions my clients had. Since then, I've gained some wisdom and want to pass along advice that can help you deal with your circumstances.

People going through custody disputes want answers about what the process looks like and what they can do to keep their children. They want to know how they can meet their children's needs and how to get through the process with as little trauma to their children and themselves as possible.

Some questions have common, across-the-board answers. For example, how does the trial work? That process is fairly similar across the country, and the answer would apply to everybody. But what about those areas that are more complicated, like dealing with an impaired spouse, a child with special needs, or a parent with a narcissistic personality disorder? How can a stepparent or grandparent fight for custody of a child? My goal is to answer these questions and more.

My goal is to help you understand that you must put your children's needs first. Although most parents know this, some need to be reminded of the unanticipated impact their actions might have on their children.

I have also written this book with lawyers in mind to give you a tool to help your clients as well as for counselors, guardians ad litem, and anyone else involved in custody situations.

Custody disputes are part of our society and are on the rise. However, armed with the right information, you will be empowered to stand up for yourself and your children, and that should be the ultimate goal.

CONTENTS

SECTION III: CHILD SUPPORT AND VISITATION

SECTION IV: PARENTAL ALIENATION

SECTION V: SPECIAL CIRCUMSTANCES

SECTION VI: TIPS FOR ATTORNEYS

SECTION I:

IN THE BEST INTEREST
OF THE CHILD

Chapter One

IN THE BEST INTEREST
OF THE CHILD

This topic is a good place to start because, ultimately, that's the goal of every custody dispute. In the context of a child custody case, the child's best interest means that all custody and visitation decisions are made with the intention of fostering and encouraging the child's happiness, security, mental health, and emotional development.

Factors That Determine the "Best Interest of the Child"

A lot has been written on what that phrase means. Googling "best interest of the child" returns 139 million results, and almost every state has defined what it means. However, it's one thing to define it, but it's something else to practice it.

What does a court look at when considering the child's best interest? When a judge determines the best interest in a custody dispute, they usually use a standard with certain factors, which can vary from state to state. They consider whether one parent presents an emotional and/or physical danger to the child, be it presently or in the future, and the mental health of the parents seeking custody. The court also considers the age of the child(ren), the geographic proximity of the parties to each other as well as the child's school, their extracurricular activities, their healthcare providers, and who has handled the children's daily needs.

Judges evaluate whether one parent is asking to separate siblings because most judges want to keep the kids together. They don't want them to change their relationship with any step- or half-siblings. They consider the plans each individual has for the child, the stability of each parent's home, and any acts or admissions of a parent that may indicate that the existing parent-child relationship is not a proper one.

After I explain these factors to my client, I want to hear them say, "Oh, okay. I have some examples where I can show each of these." Then I ask them to tell me what they are and write about them. For instance, my client could be a stay-at-home mom and the one who has always taken care of the children. Or, my client may be a dad with a flexible job that can accommodate his children's school and activities. As a result, I like my clients to go through the list and let me know their respective strengths and weaknesses.

The court typically doesn't care whether the parent has had an affair (which most of my clients find surprising), the parent's gender, their sexual orientation, or their religion. The court doesn't consider any of the parents' actions that don't directly affect the child. They are interested only in those actions that have a positive or negative impact on the child.

Chapter Two

PUTTING YOUR CHILD FIRST

Most parents know how to put their child's needs first; it's intrinsic and fundamental to parenting. Unfortunately, it doesn't always work out that way.

Parents Who Put Their Own Needs First

Every contested custody case I've handled involves a parent who can't put the needs of their children first. They either use their children as pawns, or they're so hurt by the other parent that they want to punish them. They start subconsciously manipulating situations with the children to accomplish their goals. They tell their children hurtful, toxic things about the other parent, which can lead the children to reject that parent.

Another type of manipulation is helplessness. The child is led to believe, *If I'm at Dad's, who will take care of Mom? Dad needs my love and attention, and if I don't give him that, then he's going to stop loving and paying attention to me.* That's when it really gets bad, when the kids think, *I have to give this parent my love and affection. The other parent knows I love him, so I'm safe with him. But if I don't show it to Mom, she'll cut me off like she did Dad, and then I won't have a mom.* That's a scary thing for a kid.

One of my clients was going through a separation. We hadn't had our day in court yet or come to an agreement about visitation. Her husband had a drinking problem and texted his six- or seven-year-old daughter, "Hey, I want to take you to the super fantastic bouncy house this weekend. We're going to have so much fun there." If the mom said no, she looked like the bad guy.

I don't think the father was aware of how that put his child in the middle. He also likely didn't understand how badly he hurt his child when he said, "Mommy's making Daddy leave the house right now, and I'm not going to be able to see you for a really long time."

Then there are mothers who are known to say things like, "Daddy is divorcing me and leaving us!" I don't think they thought about what messages they were sending to their children, how they thought their needs were more important than their child's ... at least, I hope not.

Where Do We Start as Parents?

The best thing you can do as a parent headed to a custody battle is to demonstrate that you're putting your child first. That's what a good parent does. It's not whether Dad was a good parent; it's about coming together as one when raising a child. It's about Dad and Mom aligning themselves and the child realizing they can't pit one parent against the other. Instead of Dad feeling sorry for the daughter, he supports the mother. He says, "Well, you've got to listen to what your mom tells you."

That's where you develop that trust with the other parent. You can call them and say, "I'm having a parenting struggle. Would you be on board with me about this?" This approach is much more beneficial for the child; you're confident the other parent will work with you instead of worrying, "Oh, if I call and tell him I'm having this problem, he is going to use it against me."

In many cases, this fear is real. Even though Mom may be doing a good job with the kids, she feels undermined and has lost confidence in her parenting abilities.

Often, a father will try to bully and manipulate a mother by telling her, "You don't know how to be a mom and take care of our kids, so I'm going to take custody from you." That's an example of a parent who can't or won't change.

Other parents, however, see the damage they could be causing their children. They think, *I really want to make changes because I don't want to hurt my kids.* They correct their behavior and become a better and healthier parent.

Be aware that a child is going to gravitate eventually to the healthier parent unless they've been destroyed by the poison fed to them by the unhealthy parent. Sadly, some children are fed so much poison about Dad that they reject him and have a relationship only with Mom, or vice versa. Then they become an unhealthy, maladjusted adult.

Brainwashing

I represented a mom who went through a divorce. Her then-husband owned several companies, and the couple was pretty well-off. The dad traveled a lot and wasn't involved with their daughter's life. The mom pretty much handled everything.

After they divorced, the mom learned that her ex-husband had sold one of the companies and had not disclosed the sale during the divorce. She filed a lawsuit against him to divide this asset and received a big sum of money for her share of that property. In addition, the judge ordered him to pay her attorney's fees.

The husband became angry. Mom had primary custody, so he tried to flip the child so she'd want to live with him primarily, and he constantly sued the mother. No sooner would we finish up one lawsuit when we were served with another one. He also tried to prevent me from representing her.

He complained that she took their daughter out of the country where they had stayed at a lovely resort. He tried to sue her again on "technicalities." The father subsequently took the daughter to the pediatrician to see if she might have contracted a disease like yellow fever or cholera or something worse that a person might get in a foreign country or from traveling down the Amazon. Yet this girl had stayed at a beautiful resort.

What happens to your child when you take them to the pediatrician? You tell the doctor, "She visited another country, and she didn't get these immunizations before she went."

Whether the fear is real or the father just wants to punish his ex-wife, he communicates to the child, "Your mom can't keep you safe." You send that unspoken message when you take her to the pediatrician's office and talk to the doctor about your fear.

Then the child starts thinking, *I'm not safe when I'm with my mom.*

Brainwashing a child doesn't do him or her any good. As they mature, they'll realize what happened. You have to rise above it and be the loving and accepting parent.

Why Putting Your Child First Matters

Many parents who don't put their child's needs first can't encourage and accept the child's relationship with the other parent. They don't want it, so they interfere with the relationship and undermine it.

I can give example after example. The parent doesn't send information to the other parent about an important event that's coming up for the child. Who does that hurt? Sure, it hurts the parent because they missed out on seeing this school event, but it really hurts the child by not having both parents there.

When I was in law school, I had a really good friend, whom I'll call Carol. She was married to Jim and divorced from Bob. Carol's relationships with these men and the behavior of Jim's ex-wife showed me the difference between what can happen when parents are healthy with their kids versus when they're not.

Carol had a healthy relationship with her ex-husband; however, Jim's ex-wife, Jane, didn't have a good relationship with him. She was constantly trying to alienate their child from Jim.

I observed that Carol and Bob, although divorced, could both attend their daughter Lisa's functions like a school play or a sporting event. They could sit together and share the moment and be friendly. Now, they weren't getting together for the holidays, but they had Lisa's best interests in mind. Any problems they had in their marriage were set aside so that they could support their daughter. The parents were flexible with each other and so forth.

Jane couldn't accept that her daughter, Sarah, would have a good relationship with her father (Jim). Jane was inflexible. Sarah was not allowed to talk about anything that happened when she was at Dad's house. When she had fun with her stepsister, Lisa, her mom didn't want to hear about it.

Jane was sending the message, "I don't want to hear about these things." Sarah learned, "I can't tell my mom these things."

Sarah loved her dad. He wasn't doing anything wrong. He was allowing her to have a relationship with her mother and wasn't trying to get back at his ex-wife. Jim made sure the clothes Sarah wore when she arrived were washed and packed for when she went back to Jane's house. Jim would say, "Okay, honey. Here are your clothes to take back to Mom," and not, "Oh, my gosh. I can't believe your mother has to have these things back." He supported his daughter.

Jim and Carol planned to take Sarah and Lisa on a Disney cruise. Because of the cruise's timing, they needed to switch one day with Jane. Jane refused to switch, and Sarah didn't get to go on the cruise.

By the time she was in middle school, Sarah was able to discern what had been happening. When Jane decided to move to Colorado with her new husband, she assumed Sarah would go with her. Instead, Sarah said, "No, I'm going to stay with Dad."

Hearing this was a real shock to Jane. I don't know if that caused her to change her ways; it probably didn't.

Eventually, Sarah figured out that Jane wasn't paying attention to her needs because she was so focused on hurting her dad. She'd say, "My mom's problem is that she doesn't like my dad. I love my dad. I want to be with him and not with somebody who makes me feel bad about the fact that I love my father."

Sarah ended up living with Jim. Many kids figure these types of things out for themselves.

Finding the Good in the Bad

Divorce and separation are rarely good for a child, but when both parents look beyond themselves and put the interests of their child first, the custody process and outcome for the child can be much less stressful. It may even force the parents to change the relationship they have with the child for the better.

When my son was four, his dad and I decided to separate. Our relationship had become nonexistent, which was part of what drove us to make this decision. We were two orbiting planets that never seemed to come together. At times I was in one room, my son's dad was in another, and my son was sitting by himself at this little table where he sometimes ate his dinner. I thought, *This is not what I envisioned for our family. Why aren't we all eating together?*

When we separated, my former husband and I wanted to put the needs of our son first; we didn't want him to be caught in the middle. We knew it would be difficult for him, so we chose joint custody with equal visitations.

One of the unexpected benefits was that I became more focused on my son, simply because I now had less time with him than when his dad and I were living together. I tried to find ways to spend more time with him. When he was at his dad's, I would go to the school to have lunch with him. I also went to a lot of sports and band practices and events.

Fortunately, I was able to step outside my relationship with his dad to meet my son's needs. When I was with him, I was cognizant of the fact that there would be days when I wouldn't see him or have him with me. I focused more of my attention on our time together. I'm sad that I didn't do that when I was in a relationship with his father, but it was one of the benefits of the separation. I think it was true for his dad too. He had to become more involved.

For my son, it took a separation for me to recognize just how badly he needed us. He lost us as parents who lived with him together, but he gained more time and focus from each of us individually that he didn't get when we were a family unit.

Chapter Three

DECISION MAKING

When parents live together, each parent has 100 percent of the rights regarding any decision related to the children. Where should they live? What doctor should they see? Where should they go to school? How should they be disciplined? Should they see a counselor, and if so, whom?

After parents separate, decision-making becomes structured differently. If they're unable to agree upon this structure, then the court will do it for them. Deciding the primary residence of the child is only part of the larger meaning of custody. Custody is a state system for deciding who will make decisions on behalf of the children and how those decisions will be made.

Decision-making can be aligned or allocated between parents in different ways. For instance, it can be given to one parent, to both parents by agreement, or to one parent after having a meaningful consultation with the other parent. A lot of it depends on the particular system in your state. Texas has a system that's based on both parents being joint managing conservators of their children. In other words, the state presumes that it's best for children if the parents make decisions together.

Most states, however, have ways for judges to make those kinds of decisions. For example, the parents might submit an agreed parenting plan that lays out those decisions and how they're going to make them. If they don't agree and the court decides which parent will make which decisions, then the judge follows the state's guidelines.

The judge considers certain factors when deciding which parent should make those decisions. He or she might look at things like whether a parent can encourage and accept a positive relationship between the child and the other parent or whether both parents participated in the child's well-being before the lawsuit. The judge considers the best interests of the child in order to weigh the children's needs, their development, and how the children benefit from the way each parent makes decisions about them.

Some states have an option where the children get to have a say in how their parents make decisions about them. Does that mean the court allows older children to decide who they're going to live with and how decisions should be made? No. And there's a lot of controversy around that right. I've had many conversations with people about children choosing which parent to live with. I think, on some level, that's putting the children in the middle of the parents.

We can still find out what a child wants, what makes them happiest, and use that as a factor but not as the main decider. Most parents don't know that. They think, *When my child gets to a certain age, they get to decide where they want to live.*

No, they legally can't until they're eighteen. In the meantime, the court has to approve any choices the child may make. For instance, in Texas, when a child turns twelve, he or she can choose which parent they want to live with, but the court only grants that if it's in the child's best interest. The court considers the child's emotional and physical needs in both the present and the future. A nursing infant has different needs than a sixteen-year-old who is more able to cope with time away from their mother.

Sometimes letting an older child choose which parent to live with can be a voluntary decision between the parents. A friend of mine married a guy from the Caribbean, and they lived in the States. When they divorced, he moved back to the Caribbean. Their teenage daughter would see him for long periods of time in the summer and maybe on holidays, but not during the week. Mom was responsible for the day-to-day care. She had to be the bad cop: do your homework, go to school, don't play so many video games, put your cellphone down—that sort of thing. When the daughter visited her dad, everything was fun in the sun.

Eventually, as children sometimes do, she said, "I want to live with my dad."

My friend let her daughter move in with her dad, who was actually a good father; he just hadn't been very involved. She said, "Let me explain something to you. If you're going to live there, that means you'll have to complete the school year there. You won't get to come home for Christmas when you decide, 'Oh, I miss all my friends.' So I just want you to think hard about it first."

The daughter responded, "Oh, yeah. I know. I want to go anyway."

The daughter was miserable for about a year. But sometimes you have to let them see for themselves that the grass isn't always greener on the other side; otherwise, they might resent you for "keeping them away" from the other parent.

Sometimes one parent is given the right to make all of those decisions. That happens in a lot in situations where either the other parent has shown they don't have the ability to make decisions with that parent, or they make poor decisions on their children's behalves.

Decision-making can also be divided up. For example, one parent makes decisions about education while the other determines medical care. Who makes decisions about what is based on what the parents agree to or what a judge decides.

Some parenting decisions will be made unexpectedly. For instance, if your child needs to go to the doctor, each parent has the right to take the child to the doctor unless the judge orders otherwise.

I had a case where the judge ordered the father not to take the kids to the doctor because he was undermining his son's medical treatment. His son had warts, something children tend to get. The pediatrician said kids usually outgrow these warts because their bodies build up an immunity. The mom decided to let nature take its course because the warts would eventually disappear.

Instead of using Mom's preferred plan based on what the pediatrician recommended, the dad made a big deal out of it. He convinced his own doctor to give him a prescription for a medication that would remove the warts. Even the pharmacist was suspicious and asked, "Did your pediatrician or doctor tell you how to use this medication? It's literally to burn the warts." The dad just said, "Oh, yeah." Then he applied this medication to his son, which caused burns on his skin. Now the father no longer has any say in medical matters for the children except in an emergency.

However, the father's ability to seek emergency medical treatment for his children is in line with the law. Because children aren't old enough to consent to emergency treatment, almost any adult can consent on a child's behalf. If you were at the scene of a terrible accident and a child needed medical care, you could consent to that. However, taking the child to the doctor is another matter, which is why parents may be restricted from seeking non-emergency medical treatment for their child.

An example would be if you're living in another state, and the child gets strep throat. Of course, you would take him to the doctor. That's different than when the child is visiting you for the summer, and you decide now would be a great time for the child to have plastic surgery on his nose. You probably wouldn't have the right to make that decision unless it was specifically awarded to you.

Sole Custody vs. Primary Custody vs. Joint Custody

The degree of decisions a parent is granted to make depends on the type of custody they are awarded based on the laws of their state.

Sole custody is when one parent has all the decision-making responsibilities and either all or a majority of the time with the children. Previously, moms were awarded sole custody, and dads got rights of visitation. The courts believed that moms were the nurturers and should have primary care of the children. Sole custody is granted less and less now and usually only happens when the other parent is deemed unfit.

Primary custody denotes who the child spends the most time with. A parent with primary custody may also make all of the legal decisions for the child. Just like with sole custody, mothers used to be given primary custody because it was assumed that the mother and child possessed a special bond. Some mothers aren't like that; some even walk away from their kids only to come back later wanting to resume their role. This may or may not happen.

In most of the situations where I've represented fathers with primary custody of the children, Mom had not been present in the children's lives, or she had serious problems with drugs, alcohol, or mental illness. I had a case in which the mom had two sons with the dad. She then got pregnant by another man and found out she was going to have a girl. She decided to move to another state to raise her daughter and only visit with her sons. She was so interested in having a daughter that she basically gave away her sons.

Joint custody can mean many different things depending on where you live. It could mean both parents make decisions and have equal visitation. It can also mean one parent makes the decisions, and one parent is just visiting.

Equal visitation can mean the child spends half of his or her time with Mom and the other half with Dad. A court can designate a primary residence, which may be necessary when it comes time to enroll the child in school. Sometimes the child lives with both parents without a legal domicile or residence allocated to either parent. They might simply say the children are restricted to living in Austin, Texas, for instance, so the child is recognized as officially living with both parents.

Chapter Four

FATHERS WHO WANT CUSTODY

When fathers want primary or sole custody of their children, it could be for any of several reasons.

First, something might be so bad with Mom that the children need to live primarily with Dad. That's typically a situation in which the mother has a serious problem like alcoholism, drug addiction, or mental illness. The children will be placed primarily in Dad's care.

Fathers may also want custody when the mom works outside the home, and he has been a stay-at-home dad. Maybe the dad can't or won't get a job. The fact is, if he has provided the day-to-day care just like a stay-at-home mom, then he's probably going to continue in that role, just as if the shoe were on the other foot. That can be hard for a working mom who questions why she should lose time with her child just because she has a job. The same can be said for the fathers.

Another reason a father may want custody is that he has a job with more flexibility, so he can be there to raise the children. He's been the primary parent, taking the children to school, packing their lunches. The children have a place to go when they're out of school.

In that situation, I ask clients to think about what's better for the children: to attend an after-school program or be with a parent who's at home? Is it better for children to be with the babysitter or with the other parent?

Because Dad may have more flexibility than Mom, he could end up with primary care of the children. I tell women in that situation the same thing I tell men: "There are ways to maximize the amount of time with your children that have nothing to do with who the primary parent is."

This could include having lunch with the children at school or attending their extracurricular activities. They have soccer practice or band practice or something that you can go and watch even when it's not your visitation. These activities allow you to have more time with your children.

Additionally, you could try to make sure that on the days you have your children, you can be at home when they get out of school. When I got divorced, my son was young. On the days he was with his dad, I worked later, and when he was with me, I picked him up from school and made sure I was there to get his homework started, and so forth.

I had flexibility with my work that allowed me to do that, but not every parent does. However, you can look for ways to maximize your opportunity to spend time with your child.

When Fathers Want Custody for the Wrong Reasons

When a father wants custody, he can't seek custody because he wants to hurt the mom. I had a dad who made fresh juice and juice smoothies for the kids, so he claimed to be the better parent and therefore should have custody. I couldn't believe how he had made this custody dispute into a serious contest. The mother was a really good mom, but he felt that because she was the one who wanted the divorce, she should lose custody of the kids. That just didn't work.

Sometimes a father will say, "I think our child should live with me primarily because Mom is an unfit parent. But I'll agree to a 50/50 visitation schedule." I'll ask, "If the other parent is so bad, why would you agree to have an equal amount of time?" In that situation, that dad looks like he's just trying to work his way to get primary custody. He doesn't really have any serious beef with Mom or her parenting.

I've seen plans like that backfire. It's a poor negotiation tactic. If you're a father seeking primary custody, you almost always are going to have to show that, in some regard, the mother is not fit to be a parent.

Changing Parental Roles

Traditionally, the division of duties have been mothers staying at home and caring for the children's day-to-day needs while Dad works. Nowadays, more and more mothers are in the workforce, and more dads are becoming involved in their kids' lives. Fathers are not just coaching their children anymore; they're going to parent-teacher conferences, volunteering in the classrooms, and engaging in other functions with the children.

More fathers want to be more involved and could be more involved. Some fathers have a greater capacity to nurture than mothers do. Changes in society are contributing to this evolution. In fact, fathers are often now in the delivery room when the baby is born, engaging in their child's life from the moment of birth.

Mothers are bringing fathers more and more into the relationship with the child. No longer does Dad work from nine to five and then have his slippers, pipe, and drink brought to him when he gets home. No longer does he read the newspaper while mom fixes dinner and gets the kids bathed and off to bed. Dad used to have a quiet evening and wasn't involved in anything except maybe going in and telling the kids goodnight.

Likewise, gone are the days where moms are automatically the chief decision-makers while dads have only basic rights and access.

That was then; this is now. Our ideas of what is best for children are changing.

Chapter Five

MOTHERS WHO ARE AFRAID OF LOSING CUSTODY

Some moms come into my office concerned about something they've heard. In their minds, it's big and could cause them to lose custody. In fact, just about every mother's fear is that she will lose custody of her kids.

In most cases, however, Dad has to prove that Mom is truly unfit to get the court to switch custody or minimize her visitation. Some men even resort to bullying or threatening Mom or lying where she is concerned. When that happens, an attorney can help by reassuring Mom that the father is only trying to scare her. In these situations, it helps to break down what the threats or the allegations are. As a mom, the fear of losing custody is so great that it can be hard to see through the threats. Having an objective person come in and rationally evaluate the threats can be reassuring.

A lot of dads threaten to take the kids away from the mother or will do everything they can to get custody. The vast majority of the time, it's just talk. Somebody who is going to get custody doesn't have to threaten you. They just do it.

Some may even try to leverage false allegations in order to win a custody case. Keep in mind that Children Services are aware that some parents try to misuse them in their custody battles. Of course, they have to entertain all allegations, but if you've done nothing wrong, they'll see it. When numerous reports are filed, which happens in some cases, it doesn't sit well with the courts to see how the other parent is abusing the system or distracting workers from the children who actually need help. No one likes to be abused.

You can prepare yourself in a few ways. First, educate yourself. The best way to do that is to meet with an attorney, even if you can't afford one. You may be able to find an attorney who will meet with you, and you can talk to them about the situation. They may be able to provide you with reassurance or guidance that, no, you're not going to lose custody of your children just because the dad is threatening you.

Arm yourself with information, identify patterns, and think about how child-care roles had been handled. Who took care of the children primarily? What are the children's daily routines? Who handled each part of that routine from the time they woke up and brushed their teeth and got out the door to school, to coming home, having a snack, doing their homework, working on projects, and so forth?

When the Mother Has a Problem

I've worked with women who are alcoholics. If that's you, you need to get sober. With clients like that, I have a conversation about what they need to do to get sober and maintain their sobriety. That may mean attending Alcoholics Anonymous meetings and having somebody sign a card to prove you attended the meetings. It may mean using a device to prove that you're maintaining your sobriety and/or submitting to regular alcohol testing. If you have had struggles in the past, you must take every step to show that the children are safe with you.

If the dad travels a lot, how serious can his accusation be if he's leaving the children in your care? That's an important point for any parent to think about when they leave the children with the other parent who's struggling with drugs or alcohol. If you ask the judge to exclude that parent from custody, it's hard to justify why you left the children with that parent for a weekend while you went out of town, but now you want the judge to prohibit that parent from having time with their children?

In that kind of situation, I ask the mother to document every time the dad left the children with her. I then present it to the court to prove that not only can she care for her children, but Dad does trust her enough to continually leave them with her.

SECTION II:

THE CUSTODY PROCESS

Chapter Six

THE CUSTODY PROCESS

When parents who are separated can't work together to make decisions regarding their children, they must enter into the custody process to resolve what becomes a battle. The degree of cooperation by both parents will dictate the time required to reach the final outcome.

The more a case is contested, the more steps are inserted into the process. However, in a basic custody case, the following is a list of steps you can use to get started:

1) Choosing an attorney:

Choosing the right attorney to represent you in a custody trial is crucial. However, it doesn't have to be difficult when you know where and how to look.

2) Attorney-Client Agreement:

Once you decide which attorney to hire, a contract will be presented to you addressing several matters between you and your new attorney, including financial terms.

3) Working with a lawyer:

Your lawyer will be your advocate in your custody case. They'll need to hear and understand your story and all its details, and then they'll strategize with you to obtain the best possible results.

4) The pleading

This petition initiates the legal proceedings for either divorce or custody or both.

5) Mediation:

Mediation is a form of alternative dispute resolution where a neutral person, the mediator, works with the parents and their lawyers to try to come to agreements regarding the children.

6) The Discovery Process:

Through this process, both sides obtain relevant information about you and the other parent that may be submitted as evidence.

7) Temporary/Interim Hearings and Orders:

Temporary or interim hearings are used when it's necessary to have orders in place while the divorce or custody case is pending. They will eventually be replaced by final orders, like a decree of divorce.

8) Trial:

When agreements can't be reached, then the next step is to have a custody trial.

9) The Ruling:

This is the end of the custody journey when the judge makes their final decision and issues their final order.

So now you're about to enter into the custody process. It's designed to be fair and just. That's why I work very hard with my clients to try to settle their cases. Although many people hire me because they're in a situation that's likely to lead to litigation, the vast majority of my cases settle without the need to go to court.

Admittedly, the process can be intimidating; it can be scary because of the unknown. But if you put your child's needs at the forefront, follow the rules, listen to your attorney or research, you *will* make it to the other side.

Chapter Seven

CHOOSING AN ATTORNEY

One of the first steps most parents need to do when entering the custody process is to choose a lawyer to draw up paperwork to formalize the custody arrangement. For many people, finding an attorney will work out relatively simply.

For those who have never been involved with family court, or any type of court for that matter, or for those who are facing issues such as alcoholism and domestic abuse with the other parent, it can be overwhelming to find an attorney who knows how to handle these special circumstances.

So how do you find a good custody lawyer?

Looking for a Lawyer Online

A lot of people today just use the Internet, which I do not recommend. If you type "best custody lawyer" into Google, you may or may not come up with good results. People and businesses, including attorneys, can word their website content in a way that maximizes search engine optimization so that their firm will come up first.

I have searched for "best custody lawyer" for my area on Google. I've never even heard of some of the lawyers who came up, and I have a relatively small community of lawyers in my town who handle custody cases. Either the lawyers who showed up in my search results are brand new, or they've figured out how to maximize the Internet to drive business to their door. They may be good marketers, but unfortunately, they might not be good lawyers.

I suggest asking friends if they know somebody who has used a lawyer to settle a custody dispute. If a friend knows a lawyer, any kind of lawyer, that can be a great start. You can ask that lawyer to refer you to someone who specializes in custody cases.

After you've gathered a list of names, do a Google search of those particular lawyers. Sometimes you can see their ranking on Google based on reviews.

However, even this process isn't without its flaws. For example, you might find a lawyer on Google who doesn't have a five-star review. That might be because the only review they have is from an opposing party who lost, and they wrote a bad review about that attorney out of spite. The review could have also come from somebody with a grudge who left a complaint anonymously.

As you do your research, keep in mind that anybody can leave a review on Google. A lawyer could have everyone in their family leave a five-star review, and then that person would be a five-star lawyer. But are they really? I don't know.

Turning to the American Academy of Matrimonial Lawyers

One of my favorite resources for custody attorneys is an organization I belong to called the American Academy of Matrimonial Lawyers, or AAML. This organization is comprised of the country's top 1,500 matrimonial lawyers, which is just a fancy name for divorce or custody lawyers.

You don't get into the AAML by merely filling out an application and paying a membership fee. Attorneys go through an extensive vetting process. They must complete an application that includes references from their peers and references from the judges they have appeared in front of. They must show they have an extensive history of trying custody and divorce cases. After the application is submitted, a request goes out to all the lawyers in the applicant's state who are in the AAML. Those lawyers are asked to do their own assessment of the attorney. They evaluate the person's ethics, skills, strengths, and so on and then indicate whether they recommend that attorney for the academy. All of this is then submitted to a committee that reviews the applicant's qualifications.

The attorney also must take the Academy's test, unless they have been tested by the state in which they practice as a specialist in law. Once the attorney has been voted on and approved by the national committee, the lawyer is invited to become a fellow.

The AAML is a much more reliable source for finding a good custody lawyer because all of its attorneys have been thoroughly vetted. They may also be the most expensive lawyers in town, charging a high rate because of their expertise and experience. That's okay; call them anyway. Most members will know other good lawyers in their town who charge a lower hourly rate. So, fellows are also a good source for finding a lawyer.

Sizing Up Honors and Certifications

A lot of states grant board certification, which means the lawyer is a specialist in his or her area of practice. For example, lawyers in Texas are given a test that was probably the most difficult exam I have ever taken. It focused heavily on divorce and custody law, so I had to show I had a deep understanding of family law issues related to divorce and custody work. To become board certified, I had to have been involved in about fifty trials and received numerous references from my peers and judges.

Then there are many services where lawyers nominate other lawyers for some great lawyer recognition. They may or may not be great lawyers. These services send emails to a list of attorneys in your state, asking them to vote whether you should be included. The rating company and process can vary from state to state, and it can be pretty rigged. Basically, it's like a popularity contest combined with a marketing strategy. I'm not saying that those lawyers aren't fantastic lawyers, but no one at those services looks into the lawyers' qualifications.

You have to be careful in assessing an attorney's honors and awards. I've heard of companies that send a lawyer an award that says the attorney is an ultimate trial or custody lawyer. It's a bogus honor from a made-up organization that's driven by a lawyer paying for a plaque. So, you really want to be wary of that.

The Attorney Interview

After you've narrowed the list down to a few possibilities, ask each attorney for an initial consultation and interview them. You'll have an hour or so to talk about your situation and get a feel for how the lawyer would handle it. Find out about this person. What is their assessment of your case? What is the process? What experience do they have? Compare and contrast the attorneys, their differences, their styles, and so forth.

Virtually every good lawyer charges for the first meeting, usually by the hour or with a set consultation fee. Lawyers charge for the consultation because it's often the most important meeting that a person will have. The meeting allows you to size up the attorney to determine if the relationship would be a good fit and if they're the type of attorney you want to hire. Everybody's wants and needs are different. Some people want a lawyer who is going to beat up the other side and be a real bulldog. Some people want an attorney with a lot of compassion and can help resolve the dispute amicably. It's a personal choice. Keep in mind that you should like the lawyer you choose because you're going to be working with that person during a very stressful time.

While you're evaluating the attorney, they're often looking at whether you're the kind of person they want to represent. When I meet with a potential client, I listen to determine whether they're interested in putting their children's needs first. I assess whether they're angry at their spouse because he or she cheated on them. If they're hyper-focused on that affair and unable to focus on the needs of their children, the person is more than likely going to use their child as a pawn to try to punish their spouse.

I also make a choice about whether I will represent someone. Not everyone who wants to hire me gets to work with me.

Chapter Eight

THE ATTORNEY-CLIENT AGREEMENT

Once you select an attorney you like, he or she will have you sign an agreement. Like most agreements, the Attorney-Client Agreement sets the terms of the relationship. It informs both parties about what they can expect from the other party and what they must do in this relationship.

The Attorney-Client Agreement is standard between an attorney and their client. However, if you have preferences you want included in the agreement, let your attorney know. For instance, you may want to communicate more frequently with your attorney, and/or you may only want to only work with the attorney, not the paralegal.

This contract outlines the lawyer's fees, their hourly rates, the terms for payment, how they charge, the billing process, when you need to replenish your retainer, other costs you're responsible for, and so forth. It also says you agree to pay the lawyer's fee as established in the agreement.

The length of an Attorney-Client Agreement can vary from one to several pages. Mine are several pages; I had started out with a one-page letter but found it only created questions or confusion. I also learned that it was smart to include issues like an arbitration clause to protect me from a potential lawsuit if someone ended up unhappy. I'm upfront about that.

My agreement also tells my clients how long they have to raise a question or dispute an invoice. It states the hourly rates of everyone in the firm and whether those rates can be raised. It states the reasons that would cause me to terminate the contract, such as the nonpayment of fees.

The terms in my agreement are not negotiable. I tell people in person and in the agreement that it's an important legal document that they should consider having reviewed by another lawyer. I welcome questions, requests, or explanations about my agreement. That shows me that someone is really looking at it, not just signing where needed and sending it back.

Chapter Nine

COSTS OF A CUSTODY DISPUTE

One of the first questions potential clients ask me is how much my services are going to cost. It depends on a lot of factors. How much time will I spend on your case? How much time will we spend communicating? Will you meet with me or call me? How difficult or easy is the other side to work with? Are there going to be disputes that a judge will need to resolve? Will we have to bring in experts? All these factors drive the cost of a case.

Unfortunately, attorneys can't tell you in advance how much it's going to cost—no one really can. Custody litigation isn't like other types of litigation, especially when it comes to costs. Whereas you can apply a financial analysis in most non-custody cases, you can't determine the value of your children; they're priceless... literally. Then it gets to what you can afford because a custody case can cost $10,000, $20,000, $50,000, or more. I've had clients who spent hundreds of thousands of dollars on a contested custody case.

At this point in the process, attorneys can only give you their rates and billing methods, which will all be discussed in detail when they present their Agreement with you. At least that can help you get an understanding of the basic costs involved in a custody dispute.

Understanding Retainers and the Cost of a Basic Case

I tell people that I am not their lawyer until they retain me. They have to sign the employment agreement or contract, and I have to accept the contract by signing it. They also have to pay the retainer, which is a deposit. It's not an estimate of how much the case will cost unless the lawyer specifically says, "This is how much I'll charge you." Some attorneys are moving toward charging a flat fee for custody cases. In most cases, though, the retainer is a deposit that the lawyer is going to bill against on an incremental hourly basis.

For example, I charge by quarter-hour increments (fifteen minutes) with a minimum of a quarter hour for everything I do on a case. I tell my clients that if they send me an email and I read it, I'm going to charge them for a quarter hour. It doesn't matter if the email took me four minutes or fifteen minutes to read and reply to it; I'm going to charge you for a quarter hour. In part, it's based on the value of my time, even if your email is a simple question. I have worked twenty-five-plus years to be able to answer that question quickly. This is why I tell my clients to be conscious of that because the fees can really add up.

I encourage my clients to save up several questions and send me one email instead of four over a few days. Then they get the most out of me for the fifteen minutes I'll charge for. It's important they handle their money wisely. Only they know how much they have to spend on a custody case.

Other Party's Responsibility for Your Attorney Fees

The other party could be responsible for your attorney's fees. It depends on whether it's a divorce where the parties are financially tied. Otherwise, getting fees can be difficult. Sometimes arguments can be made to "level the playing field" if one party has many financial resources.

Most of the time, though, the question of whether the other side is going to pay your fees is taken up at the time of trial. Sometimes awards are made. I'm conscious of building a case to support an award of fees to my clients by showing the other side unreasonably forced us to spend more on fees.

Possible Costs Associated with a Difficult Adversary

I encourage my clients to make informed decisions about how they want to handle their case. I try to do things the easy way, not the hard way. The easy way means I have a cooperative relationship with the other lawyer, and we can exchange information that each side needs through a process called "discovery." (I explain more about the discovery process later in the book.)

The hard way means the attorney on the other side is difficult to work with, or they have little control over their client. For example, when I request basic information that anybody should provide, I may have to make multiple requests, and I still may not get it. In that case, I request a hearing during which a judge will order them to turn over the information I asked for. Clients need to include these possible extra costs in their budget.

Preparing for Costs if the Case Goes to Trial

For cases that don't require additional time at the onset, the cost of a case may not be expensive on a month-to-month basis, but at some point, you may have a trial. When that happens, the lawyer will ask for a trial retainer.

Most people want an idea of how much to set aside. A lawyer can make an estimate of how many days they're going to be in trial, how much time they'll spend preparing for trial, and what the cost will be for everything that goes on behind the scenes, like putting together and/or reviewing exhibits, writing questions, and putting together other documents needed for court. All in all, the preparation can take as much time as the trial itself. In fact, for every day I'm in court, I spend at least a day preparing for that trial.

In addition to the preparation time, the court day itself isn't just the hours the attorney is in the courtroom. I spend time getting ready for trial in the mornings and even the previous nights. It can be a ten-, twelve-, or fifteen-hour day, so I multiply the hours by my rate plus any preparation time. Even with an estimate based on all of this, it almost always costs more.

And then there are things that come up that I can't control. For instance, the other side may have additional witnesses or something may take longer than anticipated.

When I give clients my trial estimates, I tell them that the estimate is just that; it's an idea of what my services might cost. I rarely say, "Oh, guess what? Here's some money back because the trial costed a lot less." That would happen if we got to trial and everybody agreed to settle, but that's a pretty rare occurrence.

Review the Attorney's Invoices

As my clients go through a case, I stress that they need to be a good steward of their money, regardless of their financial situation. A good steward reviews their attorney's invoices when they receive them and understands the charges. If they have questions about it, they contact the lawyer and ask for an explanation. They don't ignore charges that are unclear.

I'm not sure if some people ever even look at their invoices. They just pay them the same way they do their credit card statement. They think, *Mastercard says I owe $21,000. Okay, here's my check.* They don't go through their statement and carefully look at each charge to make sure it's accurate. They don't check to see if perhaps they were accidentally charged for the work their attorney did for someone else.

I want my clients to ask me questions if they don't understand something on their invoice: What is this charge for? Who was this conversation with? Why did you talk to this person?

When You Can't Afford an Attorney

Many of those who are separating from the other parent aren't in a strong financial position. What if they can't afford a lawyer? How do they represent themselves? Some people who can afford a lawyer still want to represent themselves; they just don't want to pay a lawyer.

If you can't afford a lawyer, there are services that will provide one for free. This is referred to as a "pro bono lawyer." Check with the local bar association or the American Bar Association, or do a Google search for free legal services in your area. Nearly every county and state have an organization dedicated to helping those who don't have the financial resources receive free legal assistance.

To use one of these services, however, you must meet income qualifications, and the guidelines are pretty stringent. There's a big gap between the person who might qualify for pro bono assistance and the person who can't afford a lawyer but makes too much money for free representation. In that situation, the only option is to represent yourself. The legal term for that is "pro se." You can get creative in that situation because there's a lot of resources available for people who need to represent themselves.

One resource is this book. The courthouse may have its own library with forms for virtually anything you could possibly need. You can also find resources online, but they may or may not be great. You can go to law libraries at law schools and ask for materials for people who are representing themselves. Some states even have books with the forms that people might need to file with the court and the instructions on filling them out. You can schedule consultations with a lawyer to ask them questions and get guidance without having them represent you.

I heard about a case where a woman was pretty ingenious about how she represented herself. She spent a lot of time at the courthouse watching hearings. When she thought something was applicable to her case, she would look up that file with the county clerk and find the documents that were filed in that case. Then she used them herself.

Most courthouses or libraries will have someone who can help you and point you in the right direction.

Chapter Ten

WORKING WITH A LAWYER

Once you hire an attorney, they go to work for you, not unlike any other subcontractor. There will be expectations on both sides where your attorney does what they contracted to do for you, and you have to do what you contracted to do as well. There will be communications, updates, the addressing of issues that pop up along the way, while both sides work hard to reach a satisfactory outcome.

It Starts with a Story

In the beginning, I ask my clients to write down stories and give me a timeline of what's happened through their marriage or relationship. I want a chronology, from the time they started dating to the present, and I want it in their own words. I tell them not to worry about giving me too much information because it's impossible to do that.

By reviewing what they've written, I often see patterns that the client doesn't pick up on, or I read something and can flesh out the details to capture what might be driving some of the conflicts between the parents. A chronology is one of the most helpful documents.

The Strategy Meeting

Next, I set up a strategy meeting with my client. That's when we thoroughly review the facts, the events and timeline, and my recommendations for actions.

Then the process begins. I often ask my clients to do things for me that will help in terms of my representation. In addition to the chronology of their relationship with the other parent, I ask my clients to put together a list of potential witnesses. This can include friends who know you and have seen you with your children. Other potential witnesses are people who know the children, such as teachers, daycare providers, pediatricians, counselors, and grandparents. Someone from my office will contact these people and interview them to see if they would be a good witness.

I also want to know who the other parent might call as a witness and what my client thinks they might say. That helps me prepare for court; when the other side calls their witnesses, I'll have some notes about those people.

The Pleading

The filing of the lawsuit starts with a legal document called a "pleading." It's asking the court for some relief. In many cases, this will be a petition to the court for divorce; sometimes it will be for custody. Regardless of what it's called, this document starts the lawsuit, and the other side will file an "answer" or response to the pleading.

In most states, custody and divorce pleadings are filed simultaneously. If you file for divorce in Texas, and you have children, you also have a lawsuit about the custody arrangement.

The petition is filed as Parent A versus Parent B. "Versus" means *against* and that Mom and Dad are adversaries. I ask my clients to think about that carefully before they go into court. This is a person with whom you will have a relationship for the rest of your life. When we're going to trial, a lot of my clients say they will risk not having a good relationship with the other parent because the issues involved are too important. Keep in mind, though, it's hard to pick up the pieces and move forward after the court proceedings.

This isn't like business partners who have a dispute. Here, a judge makes decisions for the business. Then the partners go their separate ways and may never see each other again. However, when you go to court in a custody case, you're going against the other parent. You're not only going to have to see them again, but you're also going to have a relationship with them until your child turns eighteen. Even after that child is grown, you may be intertwined with that parent in some way: graduations, weddings, grandchildren, all manner of life events.

Being Served Papers

If you know the other parent is filing a lawsuit against you, accept whatever papers are delivered to you. Don't try to dodge the process server (the person who delivers the court documents) because it's inevitable you'll be served. Don't be afraid of the process; it's just the formal process that has been implemented and is based on the U.S. Constitution.

When you're served with a lawsuit, don't try to read through it because even the plainest vanilla lawsuit can sound horrific to someone unfamiliar with legal writing. There can be all sorts of language in it, like an instruction not to remove the children beyond the jurisdiction of the court, a request for attorney's fees and such. Those are typical statements that are included in the initial paperwork. Share the documents with your lawyer, and let him or her explain them to you.

Don't wait to see your attorney. You'll have to respond by a certain deadline, which can be as little as three weeks after being served, and your attorney needs to know in time so that they can respond on your behalf. Failure to properly respond by the deadline can result in a "default" being taken against you. This means the judge is going to order whatever the other side has asked for in the petition, so don't delay.

The same process happens to the other parent if you initiate the lawsuit. There are a lot of ways to serve somebody, from aggressively to kindly, and you want to work with your attorney to strategize what would be best. Sometimes I simply send the lawsuit in an email to the other party and say, "Here's what I have filed on behalf of my client. Please forward these papers to your attorney, or let me know if you're going to be representing yourself."

Opting for Mediation

By filing a lawsuit, you're asking the court to determine how all those things should work. Most of my cases resolve through an alternative dispute resolution process like mediation.

In mediation, a neutral person, like an attorney or a mediator, helps both sides come to a settlement or compromise that both parties can live with. Sometimes agreeing through mediation is easier than going to court and having a judge issue a decision that is difficult for everyone to live with.

I prepare just as hard for mediation as I do for a trial. I want to give my client every opportunity to avoid the courthouse, which I consider to be a place of last resort.

During meditation, every effort is made to come to a reasonable agreement. If everyone agrees to a custody arrangement, that's wonderful. If we can't agree, a judge must decide the arrangements. Everybody needs to think about that. You need to think about what it's going to cost. You need to think about the unknown. Whenever you go to court, there is a risk that no matter how strong your case is, it might not go your way.

If you opt for mediation, several questions will be considered and hopefully agreed upon: How are we going to make decisions? Are we each going to have individual rights? Are we going to make all decisions by agreement, or is one parent going to decide after meaningfully consulting with the other parent? What are we going to do about visitation and support? Are these temporary or permanent orders?

With mediation, you have less stress, spend less time and money, and can come to a conclusion much faster as opposed to going to court. The decision-making is in your hands instead of turning your case over to a judge who will decide for you.

Preparing to Testify

From the time I start meeting with somebody until the time I go to trial with them, I ask questions and listen to how they answer. That tells me how good a witness they'll be or whether I need to spend extra time with them preparing testimony.

Sometimes people are so bad at answering my questions during rehearsal that I have an expert come in to work with them to prepare them on how to testify in court. That's a good tool to use when people are struggling with testifying. Some clients feel compelled to get their whole story in. If I ask them a question such as "Where were you born?" and they tell me all the places they've lived growing up, they're not listening to the question. That question requires the name of a city and state or a country; I don't need to hear their childhood story of living all over the country.

I want my clients to feel comfortable and prepared when they testify. We spend time talking about how to do that well. The best advice I have: always tell the truth. People who tell the truth don't have much to worry about. I also tell them to really listen to the question and answer that question, no more.

Chapter Eleven

THE DISCOVERY PROCESS

Once the lawsuit is filed, the custody case begins. You may go through a process called "discovery." This process is where your side obtains information from the other party. If you're representing yourself, you want to consult with a lawyer about how to handle the discovery process. There are many rules around objections that can be made and deadlines that must be followed.

The discovery phase can be done in a couple of ways. One is through written questions, which are called "interrogatories" in the legal world. You respond to the written questions by writing your answers, and most places require your responses to be under oath.

The other way that can be used during the discovery process is a request for production of documents. In other words, one party is asking the other to provide certain documents, such as financial records, medical records, pay stubs, and mortgage or rental agreement. Other items that can be requested are diaries (especially if you've kept a diary or journal of what has gone on during visits), calendars, phone records, bank records, text messages, emails, school records, social media documents, those sorts of things.

All discovery tools have deadlines. It's not uncommon for you to have only thirty days to respond to discovery. Your lawyer will tell you when you need to get responses to him or her. Your lawyer will also take other actions on your behalf that can include objecting to some of the written questions or obtaining extensions.

Written Interrogatories

When the other attorney sends you written interrogatories, your lawyer will let you know what questions you need to answer and what questions they'll answer on your behalf. Even if I have legal objections to the discovery, I still need my client to provide me with full answers to the questions.

One question you might ask is, "Why is it in the best interest for you to relocate to another state with the children?" I want my client to tell me every reason they can think of as to why they and the children should move, so it's a cumbersome homework assignment.

On many of the questions, I ask my clients to write full responses for whatever they want to say, and then I edit the responses in a way that I think best reflects on my client while legally complying with what was asked. It can take a lot of time, and it can be frustrating.

The questions may also make you uncomfortable, including whether you've had sexual relations with another person. If you're already divorced and you've been involved with somebody, that may not be relevant. If you've had an affair, you may have to disclose that, which can be very uncomfortable, but you have to answer all of the questions truthfully.

Request for Production

My philosophy on discovery is to give the other side what they asked for in their request for production, even if I don't think it's relevant. I can use that in strategic ways for my clients, primarily to build an argument that the other side should pay your fees.

Sometimes lawyers serve a very cumbersome request for production. It can be quite difficult to gather all these documents, but it is worthwhile to take the time to provide a complete response. A common complaint at trial is that the other party didn't produce all the requested items in their discovery. Make sure to work closely with your attorney to produce all the necessary documents.

On the other hand, we may submit the requested documents to the other side, but you can tell they're unread because they never use them in court or refer to any of its contents. I'll tell the judge about how we went through this time-consuming process. It can cost my client a lot of money, and I want my client to be compensated for that.

I also make requests for items from the other party as well. When those items come in, I have to see and review everything. I want to know everything I can about the other parent.

Supplemented Documents

Sometimes documents have to be "supplemented." This happens when discovery takes place at the beginning of your case, but the trial isn't held for six months or even a year.

Every month, you need to update the requested documents; you must supplement them. For example, if you receive bank statements each month, you need to send those to your lawyer every month. It's not just a one-and-done thing.

Social Media Postings, Emails, and Text Messages Used in Discovery

Discovery can also be done informally. In these situations, the lawyers may agree to exchange certain documents they'll need for trial. The most common items used in custody cases are social media postings, emails, and text messages. When you're communicating with the other side, always think about how your message may be seen in court. How will your response reflect on you?

Postings on social media, even if the account is private, can be obtained in a custody case. People don't think about others looking at these documents and the impact they can have. I've seen people send derogatory, hateful communications to the other party, and those are often used against them in court. The best approach is to communicate in a way that is businesslike, informational, and factual. Do not engage in name-calling or telling the other parent how to parent.

Don't try to destroy any documents or delete social media postings. If you have deleted something, let your lawyer know so they don't see it for the first time in court.

Depositions

Discovery can also include depositions. A deposition takes place when a person gives their testimony under oath just like they would in court, and you want to work with an attorney to prepare for it.

The attorney who requests the deposition starts with questions, and then the other side is given an opportunity to ask questions. However, if my client is being deposed (testifying in the deposition), I usually don't ask questions. I don't want to give the other side more information. Sometimes I'll ask questions if the other side is creating a serious misimpression; other times, I'll leave that alone. It's a strategy decision I make based on my experience, and your attorney will do the same.

The questions you'll be asked in a deposition will most likely be open-ended, so it's different than a cross-examination. When an opposing attorney takes a deposition, he or she intends to use your statements against you at trial.

Depositions are often videotaped. I have a videographer record my depositions because it adds a layer of information. It's also a little bit intimidating knowing you're going to be on camera.

When I take video depositions, the person answering the questions receives a transcript that contains every question that was asked and every answer the person gave. The transcript is created from the work of a court reporter who was present during the deposition.

Sometimes the contents of the deposition and the transcript do not come across the same as they do in a video. For example, if I ask a person a tough question and they glare at me, roll their eyes, or smirk, that doesn't show up in a written transcript, but it does show up on a video. If they take an unusually long time to answer, that won't be apparent in a written transcript either. Although videotaping is optional, it's always a better way to go.

Regardless, there is always a transcript.

Chapter Twelve

TEMPORARY/INTERIM HEARINGS AND ORDERS

Events often occur that need to be addressed right away; they can't wait for the custody trial. For instance, your client's children are currently living with her. She needs some kind of child support established now, and she can't wait three months for the trial. A temporary orders hearing will be held. That may not sound like a big deal, but it is. Temporary orders set the tone for a case.

A temporary orders hearing is just like a trial where evidence will be presented. In some jurisdictions, the court may give you as little as fifteen minutes to present that information.

Emergency Orders

Sometimes, an emergency order is needed because certain issues and circumstances need to be addressed immediately. For instance, if a parent has been involved in a car accident while drinking, we want the court to exclude that parent from having the children. Then there may be another type of emergency where the children's safety is at risk, and again, time is of the essence in protecting those children.

Non-Evidentiary vs. Evidentiary Hearings

If a temporary hearing has been scheduled, you need to know whether it's a non-evidentiary or evidentiary hearing, and so will your attorney. In a non-evidentiary hearing, the lawyers make legal arguments about whether something should happen, and no evidence is presented. In an evidentiary hearing, the lawyer has to provide evidence, such as testimony and documents.

If the hearing is non-evidentiary, sometimes you only have to attend, and your attorney will make legal arguments to the judge on your behalf. However, if you're supposed to testify, make sure you know that ahead of time. There's nothing more unnerving than when your lawyer turns to you and says, "Okay, I need you to take the stand now," and you're unprepared. It may go fine because your lawyer knows what to ask. Still, it's better to be prepared.

The court can make a temporary decision about the issues that caused the temporary hearing. For instance, the judge may order the other party to pay you a certain amount in child support until the trial. If visitation has been taken from you on a temporary order or temporary basis, that does not necessarily mean you're going to lose the case. You may have a steep mountain to climb, but your lawyer can work with you to help you get yourself in the best position possible to overcome a setback.

Don't take it too hard if you have a setback on a temporary order, especially if you're asking the judge to do something big to the other side. You may not get what you want, but that doesn't mean you won't get that outcome at the final trial; the judge just may need much more evidence. Don't be discouraged. Again, work with your lawyer to decide what steps you need to take next.

There can be more than one temporary orders hearing in a case. Temporary orders can be modified easily. If my clients are in divorce proceedings, we can see whether the visitation and the decision-making are working out between the parents or whether they need to be changed before everything is finalized. Your lawyer may have strategic reasons for wanting those sorts of orders in place.

Remember, it's a temporary order. It will eventually be replaced by another order that's agreed upon or by the judge's decision at the final trial, or it can be made permanent because it has proven to be the best arrangement for the children.

Chapter Thirteen

HIGH-CONFLICT CUSTODY CASES

Sometimes, custody cases can go on and on, putting parents in high conflict with each other over the custody of their child. These legal battles have long patterns of litigation with the potential to continue for years, especially when one parent can't or won't accept the outcome.

For the custodial parent, the other parent's never-ending barrage of motions and petitions is emotionally exhausting and financially draining. If you're in your initial custody case, that is an important possibility to think about. I caution my clients to seriously consider making agreements instead of fighting in court.

Even though I work hard with my clients to do everything we can to make sure this is the last custody case they'll ever have to engage in, for many of them, that's not possible. They're dealing with a parent who has the kind of personality that no matter how many rules you put in place, the other parent is as slippery as an eel. Rules are laid out in the order, and that order gets signed. Then the eel finds a new way to be slippery. You can get another order, and they're able to slip out of that one too.

In a high-conflict situation, entering into an agreement is tricky. Agreements are usually compromises. They may not work. If you're involved in a divorce or a case involving the children, one solution is to request temporary orders. They can be put in place while a case is pending. I usually want temporary orders to be in place for at least six months because it's a lot easier to change those orders during a divorce and/or custody case than afterward. I encourage my clients to make sure that whatever solution they end up with, whatever the final order is, that's the best it can be. It will take them through a future with their children and minimize the need to come back to court. Still, with some cases, that's just not going to work.

I've represented one client for five or six years, from the time his children were preteens until they were almost ready to graduate from high school. He was trying to gain access to his children. It evolved to the point that the children hardly ever saw him. We would get to where the relationship started building again, and then there would be another modification or Mom would start withholding the children. She literally forced him into suing her so she could come into court and say, "He's constantly suing me." She didn't include in her complaint that she was withholding the children; she wasn't following the order, and she was alienating the children from him, but she ended up looking like the victim.

In this particular case, we filed motions because the mom was truly alienating the father from their children. We weren't asking the court to step in and grant him custody; we weren't asking the court to change anything in the final order—we just wanted the court to enforce the order that the judge had established and make Mom let him see his children.

Harassment by the Other Parent

Then there are some parents who keep filing petitions and motions after custody has been established numerous times. The custodial parent has been following the order, so the noncustodial parent has nothing to complain about; they're just upset that the judge's final decision wasn't what they wanted, so they'll continue fighting even though they keep coming up with the same outcome.

These people abuse the system by using it to harass the custodial parent. They take advantage of the fact that our court system allows anyone to file a lawsuit about anything. We have to trust the judicial system will handle it, even after ten or eleven years.

If you find yourself in a high-conflict custody case, make sure you hire an experienced custody attorney and set boundaries. Hopefully, having a book like this will help people stay away from having that kind of ongoing high-conflict litigation.

Chapter Fourteen

OTHERS INVOLVED IN THE CUSTODY PROCESS

Other professionals, who are appointed by the court, will usually be involved in your custody case—guardians ad litem, evaluators, supervisors, and therapists (if the parent isn't already seeing one). Each provides their professional perspective in their area of expertise.

Counselors

A lot has been said about counseling in this book because it's part of custody and relevant in different areas of the process. However, counselors and attorneys can be like oil and water. Counselors don't like being caught in the conflict between parents. Like other people, they're afraid of the court process and being challenged by some lawyers about their work or opinions. If a counselor is needed for the children, it's good to find someone who has court experience or is unconcerned about being called into court.

If you're not already seeing a counselor, the court may order you to do so. If you are seeing a counselor, don't stop. Keep in mind that regardless of whether your counseling is voluntary or mandated, everything you say to your counselor may be subpoenaed.

Many people are concerned about their privacy and feel vulnerable about sharing their weaknesses if the other side can have access to their counseling records. They want to be able to talk about their frailties as a human being without being beaten about the head with them in court.

So, how can you see a counselor without having what you say used against you? As an attorney, I would recommend you talk with the counselor about how they could handle that. Tell them you're in a contested custody case, and you're concerned that anything you say could be revealed in court. Most counselors are aware of how to protect their patient's confidentiality by not writing everything down. They can avoid taking detailed notes and instead make short summaries of what you discussed during the counseling session.

In my view, it's better to make yourself vulnerable and get the help you need than to have problems and issues that aren't being dealt with. My experience is that judges prefer to see people get the help they need; it helps them be a better parent or co-parent.

Psychologists

Sometimes the court will appoint a psychologist to perform what is called a psychological evaluation and/or a custody evaluation. Psychological evaluations are where a court orders parties to go through psychological testing so the judge can gauge their parenting abilities and whether or not they have a mental illness.

When a parent is ordered to undergo a psychological evaluation, the other parent may worry that the person being evaluated is so good at bluffing that they will bluff their way through testing. Believe me, psychologists and people who design these tests have thought about that. As part of the design, the evaluations have questions that are asked in different ways to see whether a person is answering consistently or whether they are trying to make themselves look good.

For example, the evaluation will ask about a typical human action or habit. If a person won't admit to something every human would do, then the evaluator can tell that they're giving fake answers to look good for purposes of the testing.

In a custody evaluation, the psychologist will evaluate the entire family. This includes the parents and children and can sometimes include the stepparents.

The custody evaluator tests everybody and interviews everyone. They interview both parents several times, and they meet with the children individually. There will be a meeting with Dad and the children and with Mom and the children so the psychologist can observe interactions between them.

They'll talk with other witnesses and teachers and gather all information. They form an opinion to show how the parents' psychological makeup fits with the parenting skills and if there are problems.

When you have a custody evaluation, the evaluator will attend court. They can make recommendations to the judge regarding how custody should work, and their opinions are very important.

Guardian Ad Litem

A guardian ad litem is appointed by the court to represent the children's interests. In other words, their job is to see everything from the child's perspective.

The guardian's job can be very broad or just for a specific task, such as whether there should be a custody evaluation or whether the children need to attend counseling. Over the course of their investigation, they will talk to counselors, your children, teachers, friends, and maybe the children's doctor. They typically interview you in your home. They will speak with anyone you ask them to. They review school, counseling, and medical records.

Most guardians are skilled at what they do, but your lawyer will know the reputation of the guardians in your community. If the court doesn't appoint a guardian, your attorney will decide whether they want to have one in your case. More and more, I have wanted a guardian ad litem involved in contested custody cases. Using a guardian is a great way to admit a great deal of background information into the courtroom all at once. It's more cost-effective than if I, or even my paralegal, do the discovery at my hourly rate and interview all those people and try to get records.

Some people and professionals would rather work with a guardian ad litem than an attorney anyway; guardians are less intimidating. For example, counselors know that the guardian ad litem is approaching the situation from the child's perspective. As a result, the therapist is going to be more forthcoming with the guardian than they might be with the parents' lawyers. Additionally, if a guardian is involved, the therapist will not necessarily have to come to court because the guardian can talk about what the therapists told them.

Unlike the parents, a guardian ad litem can use what the children say in court. Repeating what someone else says is called hearsay, and rules of evidence typically prohibit a parent from repeating in court what their child says. However, the court knows that hearsay is part of the guardian's job. It's required to make an assessment.

There are dangers of a guardian ad litem using hearsay. For example, the guardian may inadvertently be subjective, get something wrong, or not stress what the therapist knows to be important. To help avoid this, your attorney needs to assess those sorts of risks. I don't take anything the guardian reports for granted unless the report comes back entirely favorable for my client.

If it doesn't come back favorable, I look at the entire file the guardian has compiled. I'll follow up with the witnesses they've interviewed, including the counselor, and make sure I'm getting the right story.

Early in my career, other lawyers told me that the judge will do whatever the guardian recommends. That never made sense to me. Guardians are humans who are susceptible to bias, or they have preset notions or experiences that they tend to overlay in their assessments. I don't hesitate to ask a guardian, "Do you agree that another reasonable guardian might come to a different conclusion?" Most likely, they'll answer yes. It's a soft way to challenge their opinions.

You should be wary if your lawyer tells you that you're going to have to do whatever the guardian recommends. That may be true in your jurisdiction, but I think it would be worth getting a second opinion, especially if the guardian has come out against you. I've been successful many times in getting courts to do something different than what the guardian recommends.

I had a client with a disability, and the guardian raised the concern about the mom not being able to comfort her children if they were bullied. The guardian questioned how the mom could help them with their homework. I asked my client about what she would do in certain situations, including those the guardian raised, and she had a plan and resources.

I was able to disagree with the guardian's recommendation and still show her respect. Ultimately, the judge didn't accept any of the guardian's recommendations, which was a huge win for us.

In working with a guardian, you have to remember they're not your friend; they're a professional who's been appointed by the judge. It's important to be honest with them and to answer their questions candidly. Your attorney should work with you for your meeting with the guardian so you can have relevant documents and information that can be easily conveyed to them.

On the other hand, don't hesitate to ask the guardian for help. For example, you can say, "I'm having a hard time communicating productively with the other parent. What do you recommend I do, or what can I do to handle this conflict better?" They may be able to give you recommendations to improve the situation.

Another example is if your child is misbehaving. You can say, "I'm really worried about my child. I can't seem to manage his behavior.

What can I do?" That shows the guardian you're interested in doing what's best for your child. Don't try to cover up your struggle and pretend like you can manage your child's behavior. Ask the guardian for help and recommendations.

In the course of a custody case, people are afraid to be vulnerable and expose themselves. I always go back to: vulnerability + requests for help + action = success.

Home Study Evaluator

A home study is very similar to part of the investigation a guardian does, but in some states, it can be done by a social worker, custody evaluator, an attorney specializing in home studies, or a private organization. In a home study, this evaluator comes into your home to do an investigation. They want to see what your home looks like. This may include inspections of your refrigerator and pantry and will most certainly include the kids' rooms.

They'll spend a couple of hours or more in each parent's home and observe the interaction between you and the child and how you handle things. They're aware that their presence may have some impact on the interactions, so don't worry about that. Just try to carry on with your normal routine.

The Report

The jobs of all of these people—counselors, guardians ad litem, court-appointed evaluators, and home study evaluators—are to prepare a report to submit to the judge. Any or all of these individuals could be called as a witness, usually at trial. It's important that your attorney review the entire report, and it's just as important that you review it as well so that you can talk about any problems you might see in it.

If any of these experts make a recommendation to the parents, they must follow it. Their willingness to follow recommendations, even if they're not favorable to you, reflects positively on them as a parent.

Chapter Fifteen

THE TRIAL
Preparation: The Key to
Winning in the Courtroom

Either the court or the attorneys set the case for trial. Scheduling a date three to six months out would not be unusual, so you should be notified in plenty of time.

It's a good idea to talk to your attorney before going to court and learn step by step what happens. Every jurisdiction has some differences in the way their courts are run.

On the day of the trial, you show up either with your lawyer or alone if you're representing yourself. All the steps you've taken, all the hoops you've jumped through, all the sleepless nights and stress-filled days have come to this...the trial. This is the culmination of the past few months or years, where finally, your voice will be heard by the judge, the one person who will make the final decision on the custody of your child.

In this chapter, I'll discuss more specifically what happens once the trial starts and you get inside the courtroom. I hope to answer any questions you may have as to what a custody trial looks like.

Inside the Courtroom

Everything inside the courtroom is designed to let you know this is a serious place. The space is designed to be a little bit intimidating so you know the events that happen here matter. It's designed to make you aware of where you are.

You enter through the gallery where the public sits and then cross through a barrier or partition called the "bar" that separates the audience from the rest of the courtroom.

At the very head of the courtroom is the bench where the judge sits along with their court reporter and sometimes other staff. The witness chair is on one side of the bench.

Facing the bench are the tables where each side sits with their attorney. The attorneys or their paralegals will set up their files for the trial. Don't be surprised if the attorneys are pleasant or even friendly with each other. They're not enemies. They'll have many, many cases with each other over the years, and it benefits their clients for them to have a professional, cordial relationship. It doesn't affect their advocacy for you.

When at the counsel table, your attorney sits on the side that allows them to stand up easily to make objections, to approach the witnesses, and to walk into an area that's called the well. It's located in front of the judge.

I always have a paralegal who assists me in court, but not all attorneys do. The paralegal hands me exhibits, and they're also my eyes and ears for other things going on in the courtroom. I prefer to concentrate on the questions I'm asking and the answers people are giving me.

Once the attorneys are set up, the judge enters the courtroom from behind their bench. A bailiff announces their entrance by telling everyone to rise. No one sits down until the judge gives permission. When the judge leaves to take a break, everybody stands up. Again, nobody moves away from the table until the judge has left the courtroom. It's a sign of respect.

Special Master/Magistrate, Private Judges, and Arbitrators

There are times when the court may assign a special master or magistrate to preside over your trial. This person is empowered by the judge to make certain decisions. For example, they might hear disputes regarding the discovery process. They might even hear the case and make recommendations to the judge, and then the judge makes a decision based on that recommendation. Having a special master or magistrate varies from place to place.

Some jurisdictions allow the use of a private judge. This is a retired judge who is paid to hear your case. What's great about using a private judge is that the proceeding is private, and access to the judge is much quicker than most court systems.

Arbitration is another way to resolve the case. An arbitrator makes a decision after hearing evidence. It's like a private judge except that the arbitrator may be an attorney or someone else trained in the arbitration process.

Courtroom Etiquette

When in a trial, consider that all eyes are watching you for cues to your character and about you as a person. Your body language and actions can cause favor or disfavor, so it would behoove you to make sure you come across in the right way.

Make sure you dress appropriately because it reflects your respect for the court. I've seen people come to court wearing blue jeans and flip-flops. That's not appropriate. I wear a suit, but my clients don't necessarily need to wear one. Men don't have to wear a jacket and tie, but they should wear nice slacks and a nice shirt. Women can wear slacks or a skirt and a nice blouse or a dress. You should be dressed a little nicer than you would if you were going out to a nice restaurant.

I've had clients worry about having tattoos. The judge isn't influenced by a smattering of tattoos, but they might be influenced if you have tattoos from head to toe like a tiger. It will create a certain impression or bias about you. It's just an added layer to overcome, but it can be done.

Like most attorneys, I'm familiar with most of the people who work in the courthouse. My clients need to realize that they're not going to know whether somebody they see in the hall is the judge (if they haven't been to court yet), the staff attorney, a person involved in another case, or the judge's clerk. They must be on their best behavior and act like they're standing in front of the judge at all times. If a client conducts themselves inappropriately, they need to be mindful that someone may tell the judge about their behavior.

Clients shouldn't talk about their case with or around other people in the courthouse. Some jurisdictions prohibit you from engaging other people who might be witnesses for your trial. You should ask your attorney if you need to be aware of any special rules when you go to the courthouse.

The judge's primary job is to assess the credibility and truthfulness of every witness, so it's imperative that you be on your best behavior in the courtroom as well. It shows that you respect not only the judge but the judicial process. Everything that's happening in the courtroom, everyone's behavior, and everyone's demeanor, all of it's being picked up by the judge and their staff. Thus, eye-rolling, heavy sighing, outbursts, writing notes in a dramatic manner, or even playing a game on your phone are strictly off limits.

Don't smirk at the other parent in the courtroom or try to stare them or other witnesses down if they're on the witness stand. If something like that is happening, I'll often make a remark to the judge.

I've had witnesses try to stare me down, and it's uncomfortable. They're trying to intimidate me, and it's a bullying tactic. I don't intend to break my gaze from that person, so I stare as if I'm looking through them. It breaks their concentration, and then I'm able to look away. I don't worry about what they think, even if they believe they've won when I look away.

When you're on the witness stand, try to be as relaxed as possible even though you're in a situation designed to make you feel intimidated and uncomfortable. Sit in a comfortable position. Fold your hands in your lap.

Know how to interact with the judge. If the judge asks you questions, make eye contact with the judge and answer them. I've heard lawyers instruct their clients to turn to the judge and tell them why they want their children. That's not an effective form of advocacy, and judges don't like it. Even at the end of the case when the judge gives a ruling and is typically looking at you and communicating to you, don't talk to the judge unless they solicit you.

Judges have heard every parenting story, including the worst of the worst where parents have physically abused their children in the most awful way. You want to keep the judge's perspective in mind and not go in and complain about the other parent being unfit.

On the other hand, you'll probably hear the other parent say things that won't make you happy. They may be exaggerations or even outright lies. Wear a "poker face," and don't give away your reactions.

Be careful not to feel pressured to tell the judge the whole story. A trial is like a jigsaw puzzle. It takes many different pieces to put together that picture for the judge. The judge may not be able to see the whole picture by looking at or hearing just one piece of it. It's similar to my handing you a piece from a jigsaw puzzle, even if it only has ten pieces. You may not know what the entire picture is. Sometimes my client's testimony will be the smallest piece of the puzzle. The bigger piece is going to be records or expert testimony or emails or some other type of evidence.

Treat everyone in the courtroom with respect, including the other lawyer, even if they're being disrespectful. It's the other attorney's job to ask you hard questions that challenge your views and your testimony. Be prepared for that.

Don't engage in a debate with a lawyer. Even the worst lawyer has been trained in debate and how to ask questions, so arguing with the other lawyer will never end well for you. It's also disrespectful to the court. If the lawyer is being disrespectful, the judge is noting it. Answer their questions calmly. You can even say, "I don't see it that way," or "I don't agree with your view," and then leave it at that. Don't answer their questions with questions. Make sure your behavior is beyond reproach, and always be polite.

Trust your attorney to deal with the other lawyer's conduct. If they're badgering the witness, it's your attorney's job to tell the judge to redirect the other lawyer. Sometimes the judge will do that on their own.

It's okay to show human emotions in the courtroom. Sometimes my clients are worried they'll shed some tears. It's fine to be a human being when you're on the witness stand. The judge can tell the difference between people who are truly emotional and people who are dramatic and trying to make themselves upset to stress a point or be manipulative. The latter is not a great tactic. So, if something causes you to cry, go ahead and cry. The judge will allow you to have some tissues and a sip of water, and if you need a moment to compose yourself, you can ask for it.

When in court, you'll be given break periods called recesses. During this time, you may go out into the hallway, use the restroom, and confer with your lawyer. Just remember that when you're walking around in the courthouse, the judge's eyes are on you.

Opening Statements

A trial starts with the attorneys giving an opening statement, which is a brief outline of what the facts are and what the party, or the parent, is going to ask the judge to do.

I tend to start by giving the judge some basic background information. It's not unusual for the judge not to know anything about the case they're about to hear. I always give the judge a basic chronology and the essential facts of the case. I state whether the parents are married, when they got married, when they separated, how many children they have, the children's names and ages, and where they go to school. Then I state their current status, such as they're now seeking a divorce, and tell the judge a little bit about what has caused this family to split.

Most importantly, I inform the judge about the relief we're requesting from the court, which is what we're asking the judge to do. I may say, "We're asking you to make Mom the primary decision-maker for the children and give her the right to determine where they live. She wants to move out of state. Here's what we have in mind for visitation and what we're asking in terms of support."

I can't tell you how many times I've asked the other parent what they're asking for in terms of visitation, and they don't have an answer; they don't know. Your attorney needs to help you come up with the relief you're asking for. You need to agree to and understand what you're asking the court to do and why you're asking it to make certain orders for visitation or support or custody.

An opening statement is not the time for me to advocate for my clients; however, I sometimes give the judge a preview of what's going to happen. I'll say something like, "We expect the evidence to show how the father has a serious alcohol problem," or briefly state whatever the situation is.

As the other attorney gives their opening statement, I take notes. Attorneys sometimes overpromise what they can't deliver, and/or stretch the evidence, or they'll make a broad generalization that I'll be able to show not to be true. I pay attention to what the other attorney is asking for because I'll often ask the opposing party questions during their testimony based on something their attorney said in the opening statement. I'll repeat it to the other parent and say, "You know that's not accurate because here are the emails that show otherwise."

Calling the First Witness

Once opening statements are given, it's time to present evidence to the court. Evidence consists of individuals' testimonies; people don't often realize that what is said is evidence. It also consists of trial exhibits, which are documents that will be seen by the judge. Throughout the trial, the judge needs to see and hear evidence in order to make a decision.

The side that filed the lawsuit goes first. They usually call the plaintiff or petitioner, but they can call anyone to the witness stand they want, including the opposing parent. I like my clients to be prepared in case that happens. It's disarming if you think the other side's going first, and you're going to get to hear all of their evidence.

Then all of a sudden, you're the first person called to the witness stand.

At times, I call the opposing party as my first witness. It's a very specific strategy I have in mind for the case, but I rarely use it. I employ this strategy when I have a lot of documents that I can use against the other person, such as emails and text messages. Maybe they've been deposed. This information allows me to cross-examine that person before they get a chance to tell their side of the story.

The usual flow is that the attorney calls their client to the stand and then any other witnesses, such as friends, neighbors, teachers, counselors, doctors, experts, and other people and professionals. Under direct examination, the attorney will ask those witnesses questions. The questions are usually open-ended and start with who, what, where, when, why, and how. They're designed to let the person explain a little bit about the situation.

Cross-Examination

Once the attorney has finished questioning the witness, the other attorney has an opportunity to ask questions. That's called a cross-examination. I spend time with my clients beforehand, explaining how to answer questions on cross-examination.

During a cross-examination, the lawyer for the other parent will ask questions similar to what you hear on TV: "Isn't it true that...?" "Isn't that accurate?" For example, the attorney could ask, "Isn't it true that on Tuesday you picked up your children late from school?" The argument is whether it was Tuesday. The answer to the question is no. I want my clients to be careful not to be disingenuous and give the full answer, which would be, "It was Wednesday, but yes, I did pick them up late." I also tell them it's okay to say no since it was Wednesday, not Tuesday.

These questions are not open-ended but designed to be answered with a yes, a no, or an "I don't know." People are afraid to say, "I don't know," or "I don't remember." It's okay to not know and not remember. It's okay to say, "I don't remember those specific dates." No judge expects a person to have a perfect memory.

Know in advance that you won't be able to explain your answers when the other attorney cross-examines you. If you try to do this, the judge may turn to you and say, "The lawyer is asking you to answer either yes or no."

It's uncomfortable but just answer the questions. Your lawyer will find a way for you to further explain your answers.

He said/she said

My clients often express concern about the trial becoming a case of he said/she said. Welcome to the land of custody cases. That's what it's all about: he said/she said. Often what happened in the home was witnessed by only two people: the parents. One person is going to say one thing, and the other person is going to offer another version.

My client will say, "My spouse (or the other parent) is a really good liar, and they always get away with it." I tell them that they're going to be in a different situation where lying doesn't work. Liars will lie about something insignificant in the courtroom, and they'll get caught. It undermines their entire credibility. The judge will assume that if a person lies about something small, they'll lie about something big, so it's important to be honest.

Instead of engaging in he said/she said, I like to give the court concrete examples of what happened, even in situations where the other parent was the only other witness. Talking about the event using sufficient details and showing examples like text messages, emails, or pictures is easier than relying on he said/she said when it comes to proving your point.

We don't offer conclusions to the judge. If the other parent is a bully, let the judge come to their own conclusion. We merely reveal a person as a bully by listing examples of their acting that way. We describe their actions and their behavior, and I might ask my client where the other party was standing or to describe the tone of his voice regarding a specific incident.

Then my client responds, "He got right in my face and used loud voices. I was backed into a corner." That tells the judge a lot more than saying, "He bullied me."

Making your statements

Whether you're testifying at a deposition or in court, and a court reporter is present, keep in mind that the court reporter can only transcribe one person at a time. For example, when my client and I are conversing, we often talk over each other. By the time you get midway through your question, I already know what you're going to ask me, so I start to answer you. You can't do that when there's a court reporter.

If you talk over the lawyer or the lawyer talks over you too much, you're likely to get a reprimand from the court. Even when you know what the question is, wait until that person has stopped talking. That can be hard to do, but waiting shows respect to the court and the court reporter. Of course, you may forget if you're nervous, and it's okay for a judge to sometimes remind you of these rules. Don't take it personally.

In a conversation, you may say, "Uh-huh," and I know you mean *yes,* or you may say, "Uh-uh," and I know you mean *no,* but those sounds get transcribed the same way as they're said. I'll ask, "Was that a yes?" and keep asking until they catch on and start saying "yes" to make the record clear. Otherwise, people can't tell what those sounds mean when reading a transcript.

Take Responsibility

Let's say your spouse recorded you shrieking at him. Believe me, judges are human too. They know parents sometimes argue. It doesn't mean anything is wrong or bad about them; they just had a terrible disagreement. All kinds of things could have impacted that parent on that day.

If the other lawyer is playing a recording of you screaming at the other parent, and you're listening to it, take responsibility. You can say, "Yes, that's me. No, that was not my best day. I regret that behavior, and I've tried to take steps not to do that again." Your lawyer can help you prepare to handle difficult moments like that.

It's normal to feel defensive, but blaming the other parent and claiming they were goading you doesn't reflect well on you when you're on the witness stand. I've had people who took drugs say, "The other parent did it too," to which they were told, "We're not talking about the other parent right now; we're only talking about you."

When you try to deflect the point away to the other parent, you're not taking responsibility for your own conduct. Instead of deflecting, you can say, "Yes, on that occasion, I did smoke marijuana, but it's not something I regularly do. I understand how this has impacted me in this case, and I'm sorry."

Balancing honesty with too much information

Although honesty is crucial, keep in mind you're not going to confession where you have to tell everything. Only answer the questions that are asked of you; give only the information solicited. If there's something unfavorable in your case or about you, you don't have to offer it up in your quest to be honest. It's the other lawyer's job to elicit that information from you.

If something negative happened in your past, like you were arrested once for driving while intoxicated, you don't have to tell the other lawyer that unless they ask you that question specifically. You're still being honest, but you're not required to confess this on the stand. That's not the way it works.

Telling the truth is the number-one rule when testifying. An honest person doesn't have anything to hide.

Then once you're done testifying, oh happy day!

The Judge's Chambers

During trial, it's not unusual to hear the judge say, "I want to see the lawyers in chambers." Be prepared for that. All of a sudden, your advocate disappears into a room with the other lawyer, and you don't know what's happening. It can make you feel uneasy.

The judge sometimes calls the lawyers into chambers because they see a possibility for the lawyers to work something out. They might give the lawyers some direction.

Trust that your lawyer is going to advocate for you and that they will tell you what the judge said upon their return. I tell my clients exactly what happened when I was in chambers, even if it's news they may not want to hear or that I may disagree with. At least we're going to know what steps to take.

Closing Arguments

Once each side has put their witnesses on the stand and both attorneys have had the opportunity to ask questions of the witnesses, the trial is done. At that point, a judge may ask the attorneys to give their closing arguments, which is their opportunity to advocate for their clients and tell the judge why they want the relief they're requesting.

During closing arguments, your lawyer explains to the judge in a powerful speech why they ought to rule in your favor. It's a great opportunity for my clients to see me fight for them and tell their story in a strong summary. Not every judge allows a closing argument, and more often than not, the closing argument in and of itself won't persuade a judge. However, it's not impossible. I have, once in a blue moon, seen the judge change their mind and become convinced by what was presented in the closing argument.

One of my best strategies is to treat every one of my trials like I'm preparing a closing argument, and I use my closing argument throughout the trial. I want the judge to clearly see what the situation is and what the obvious remedy is. If I've done a good job laying out the evidence and telling my client's story, I don't need to do a closing argument. I've already put everything the judge needs to know in front of them so that they can make the decision that's best for my client.

Sometimes there may be a complex issue, and the judge will want briefs submitted. Briefs are legal writings and case law, which can help the judge make a decision. Typically, though, judges are quite experienced in hearing family law matters and understand what the law is regarding the issues in your case.

The Ruling

Naturally, going through a custody trial is nerve-wracking because you don't know what the outcome will be. It's scary when you don't know what's going to happen, and you're putting your life and the lives of your children in the hands of a judge you don't know and who doesn't know you. It's normal to be fearful. It's also a lack of control. You can't control the outcome.

Overall, judges try to do what is best for children. They try not to let their own biases or experiences influence them; instead, they try to make their decision based on the evidence, but they're human beings too. Their own lives and experiences can affect them. If you have a judge who grew up with an abusive and dangerous alcoholic parent, they might be more inclined to limit custody or visitation than a judge who has no experience with that and believes that when somebody makes a promise not to drink to the judge, they're going to keep it and follow the judge's order.

In custody matters, the judge has made up their mind based on the evidence they've heard, usually before the last witness testifies. It has been my experience that judges don't often take things under advisement or rule on another day. Frequently, the judge will give an oral ruling at the end of the trial while we're all in the courtroom. They don't even write anything down at the time. As soon as the judge speaks the ruling, that is the order of the court; the order is in place. The attorneys need to make sure they understand what the judge says. Unless the judge says this will happen on a date in the future, it applies right then and there.

The lawyers then take the ruling and put it into the form of a written order, typically a page or less of notes, but the written order itself can be many pages long. For example, a judge in Texas might order joint managing conservatorship, standard possession and guidelines child support. Those few words translate into many pages of an order detailing everything that goes into defining those terms. The attorneys will then submit that written order containing the judge's rulings to the court for signature.

The client should read the order as the attorney drafts it, making sure they understand it. Rulings and orders are not fun documents to read: they're lengthy and complex, but they're some of the most important documents you'll have in your life. Be sure to read them, and ask your lawyer questions if you don't understand something.

Always follow the order that a judge makes, even if it's not in your favor. If a judge says he wants you to wear a silly hat on Tuesdays, wear a silly hat on Tuesdays. Failure to follow a judge's orders can result in what's called contempt, which means you can either pay a fine or go to jail.

Appealing the Order

Rulings can be appealed if they're not favorable to you. Your lawyer will guide you on whether an appeal is something you should pursue. In most jurisdictions, though, family law judges have broad discretion to make decisions, and it's very difficult to overturn them. It's not impossible, though, and it does happen.

SECTION III:

CHILD SUPPORT

and

VISITATION

Chapter Sixteen

CHILD SUPPORT

Child support is a payment from one parent to the other to cover the cost of expenses incurred while raising the child, such as food, medical expenses, clothing, school supplies, sports, and even activities such as trips to the zoo. It ensures that both parents take responsibility and participate in the financial portion of raising their child.

Calculation of Child Support Amount

Every state has its own way of calculating support. It can be very specific and very different. You should talk to a lawyer in your state or look at state resources to see the calculation method. Essentially, child support is based on the income of either the paying parent or, in some states, the income of both parents combined.

For example, in Texas, the person's net employment income (how much they make after taxes), or minimum wage if they're not employed, and other income is added together. That amount is multiplied by a percentage based on the number of children who need to be supported. If it's one child, the child support amount is twenty percent of the paying parent's net income. The more children, the higher the percentage. Texas caps the payment at a certain amount.

If you're wealthy, support will be calculated in a different way. You might pay child support based on the proven needs of your child. If you earn half a million dollars a year, the standard child support calculation will probably not be used, because it looks more like a division of a person's property than of an amount needed to support a child.

Insurance for the Child

Child support also includes provisions to make sure children have health insurance. One parent will be responsible for providing health insurance. The parents will then split the costs not covered by insurance. That could be a co-pay or the cost of surgery. That's considered child support as well. If the parent doesn't pay their portion of the child's medical expenses, they are considered to not have paid child support.

Refusal to Pay Child Support

Some parents don't want to pay child support; in fact, they don't believe the receiving parent deserves to get the money for whatever reason. Maybe they're angry at the other parent for having an affair and want to punish them. Maybe they think they shouldn't pay since they don't have custody of their children.

They might think the other parent will take that child support and spend it on themselves. I tell them, "I don't care if the other parent cashes the check, goes to Nordstrom and spends the money." There's a trickle-down effect in that household with other money coming in. Whatever that parent does with the child support check doesn't matter. Do the children have a roof over their heads and clothes on their backs? Are they going to school? Do they have shoes? Okay, then. That support is helping with that. The parent who's receiving support doesn't usually have to provide proof of the child's expenses and show receipts.

Child Support and Visitation

Many people have the misconception that if the noncustodial parent doesn't pay child support, then the custodial parent doesn't have to let him or her see the children. It's a common tit-for-tat, and it's wrong.

If you don't let the children see the noncustodial parent, you can be in as much trouble as the parent not paying child support.

The concept in the law is called "Clean Hands." You must have clean hands when you come to court. If you have withheld the children because the other parent didn't follow the orders, you have nothing to complain about.

Let the judge take care of making sure the other parent does what they're supposed to do. Don't try to fix things yourself. It could cause you more problems.

Help Collecting Child Support

The state has an interest in making sure parents are paying their child support because it keeps a child off public assistance. Every state has an attorney general who is responsible for state lawsuits, which include enforcement of child support laws. Therefore, a parent who is supposed to receive child support can ask for help and not pay a lawyer to do child support enforcement. Additionally, the state's attorney general looks at whether the payments should be increased or decreased.

Many tools are available to collect child support. Some states suspend nonpayer licenses such as driver's licenses, medical licenses, hunting licenses, and so forth for nonpayment of child support. In some states, you could have a lien put on your house. Gambling gains and tax refunds can be intercepted. In fact, a lot of people get their child support as the result of a document being filed and sent to the IRS; the IRS then sends the nonpaying parent's refund to the other parent.

You can also be arrested if you don't pay child support, unlike other debts that go unpaid. You could go to jail for six months at a time. The downside is that if the parent is in jail, they're not working and earning income. How can you collect child support from that parent? It becomes a very complex problem.

I've had a situation where somebody was told he was going to jail until he paid the child support. It was clear the person had access to money. Lo and behold, as soon as he was booked into jail, he paid the amount he owed his children's mother. He spent only a matter of moments in jail, but it got her the check.

Child Support in 50/50 Visitation

A lot of people think that if they agree to a 50/50 visitation, they don't have to pay any child support. That's not necessarily correct because again, visitation and child support are separate issues.

If you are in a 50/50 situation, support can be calculated in a lot of different ways. The higher-earning parent might still pay the full amount of child support in recognition that the other parent is taking care of the day-to-day expenses and paying fees for school photos and extracurricular activities.

The judge might also look at the amount of child support each parent would pay to the other and then offset it. That way, if one parent's child support obligation is $500 and the other parent's is $700, then the parent with the $700 obligation might pay the other parent the $200 difference.

Another scenario is that neither parent pays child support, and they split the expenses. That's great if the parents can get along; not so much if you can't.

In rare circumstances, a parent might be ordered to pay all the children's expenses. I had a client who had a medical condition, and the father was ordered to pay all the expenses related to the children, every dime: their clothes, their school supplies, and so forth. My client didn't have the ability to hold a job. The money she had was limited, and it had to last for her entire life. The court recognized that the father made a lot of money and had the ability to pay for all of the children's expenses. The judge chose not to burden the mother with having to pay those expenses.

In this case, the court's decision was the right and fair thing to do.

Chapter Seventeen

VISITATION

Every state has its own visitation format. Most places have a system that involves a midweek visit and/or weekend visits.

50/50 Visitation

Parents often enter into a 50/50 visitation plan agreement. It can mean the same as joint custody or that parents have equal decision making and a visitation schedule.

A 50/50 visitation plan works best when parents live relatively close to each other. It can be a week on, a week off, for example. It can also involve a division of days during the week so that one parent always has Mondays and Tuesdays with the children, and the other parent always has Wednesdays and Thursdays. Then they alternate weekends. That's referred to as a 2-2-5-5 plan because one parent has the children for two days, and the other parent has the children for the next two days. Then, starting on the weekend, one parent will have the children for five days (Friday through Tuesday), and the other parent will have them for five days (Wednesday through Sunday) the next weekend. It's easy to see if you look at a calendar.

When I divorced my son's father, he was a pretty involved dad. I had started my law practice and had to work long, hard hours, and he was super supportive. One of us drove our son to school and dropped him off, and the other picked him up. My son's father did a lot of things that were helpful.

When it came time for us to separate, I knew he could take good care of my son, and he loved him. My son was four at the time, and we agreed to a 50/50 visitation.

Still, it was hard for my son. He had a strong preference for me, but not because his dad wasn't completely competent at what he was doing. Looking back, we should have taken my son's bond with me more into consideration.

For a long time, my son went through this phase where, when he was with me, he wanted more time with me, but he also missed his dad. When he was with his dad, he missed me. He was in a situation where he really couldn't win and get all of his needs met.

As he grew older and I wasn't living in the neighborhood any longer, Dad remained where my son grew up. I could see that my son had friends there. He was in the marching band and played football at the local middle and high schools. I lived farther away, which required a long drive. Sometimes he spent more time with Dad.

A part of me was afraid that one day he would say, "Mom, I really want to stay with Dad during the week and come visit you on some weekends." I tried to prepare myself for that because it would have been in his best interest, but he never did. I would have missed him, and I would have longed for time with him, but that would have been best for him. Looking back, I can see I spent a lot of time worrying about having less time with him, but I had learned to focus on the time we had together.

A 50/50 visitation was best in my situation. More and more courts are starting to move in the direction of 50/50 visitation, believing that's what's best for kids.

Supervised Visitations

If we show the court that a parent has a drug or alcohol problem, other behavior problems, or is violent, we can ask that visitation be supervised. Supervised visitation is when a third party supervises the time between a child and a parent.

The person who supervises these visitations can be someone both parties agree to, but I prefer to have therapeutic supervision where a person trained at supervising visits is present during the visitation. They're allowed to intervene and redirect the parent if necessary, guiding what they can and cannot say to the children.

The person providing the supervision is going to be an important witness because they are the eyes of the court on what happens during visitation. Did they have to redirect the parent? How did the parent handle that redirection? How involved is the parent with the children? Did the parent just observe, or did the parent interact with the children? The person supervising observes and reports what happens because we don't want to put children in a situation where they can't protect themselves.

You may have a hard time convincing a court that supervised visitation is required. I've had cases where a parent didn't want to be supervised, so they skipped the scheduled visits with their children. At that point, the judge had to decide what to do. If you don't see your children during supervised visits, you're not likely to convince a judge that you should have unsupervised visits with your children.

If you've been given supervised visits, certain situations may cause you to sometimes jump through hoops to re-establish trust with the court. For example, if you've been arrested for a DUI with your child in the car, you'll be prohibited from driving the children for a while. Then you'll need to prove to the court that you can drive and keep those children safe. You may have to use a device that proves you're sober when you get in the car. Each time you start it, you have to blow into this device to test your alcohol level, showing that you're sober. After a certain amount of time, a judge can say, "Okay. You've done it often enough that I'm going to the next level. You still have to blow, but you'll be able to take your children in the car with you." If you say, "Well, I'm not going to blow," then you'll never be able to drive your kids.

These are some of those hoops. If a judge says you have to have supervised visitation, it behooves you to follow the order so that you're re-establishing trust, even if you think it's wrong. If you don't go, then the judge thinks, "Is getting your way more important than the safety of your children?" That's what you communicate to the judge when you don't follow a supervision order.

Sometimes the hoops are warranted, and sometimes the hoops don't seem fair or right. Either way, those were the hoops that were put in place, so you must jump through them.

SECTION IV:

PARENTAL ALIENATION

Chapter Eighteen

PARENTAL ALIENATION

One of the issues on the rise regarding custody is parental alienation. In fact, according to my website designer, it's the most popular search term related to child custody.

Parental alienation is when one parent tries to keep their child from the other parent. Either they physically take the child away and refuse to let the other parent see the child, or they manipulate the child into not liking or fearing the other parent, so the child doesn't want to have a relationship with that other parent.

Parental alienation becomes a matter of the favored parent versus the rejected parent. The children favor one parent and reject the other. The question often boils down to whether the rejection is rational or irrational. If the children had a good, loving relationship with Dad while the parents lived together, but now they have weak reasons for not seeing Dad, then the rejection is probably irrational.

I've never represented a parent who was alienating their children. I've represented the parent who is the non-favored parent. I like to wear the white hat; I want to represent the good guys. I always want to represent the side that cares about the children and is putting the children's needs first. The examples in this chapter are of mothers alienating the children from the father, but a father can alienate children from the mother just as easily.

I had a client who had lived in another country with his wife and two children. He was supposed to be away for his job but returned home earlier than expected. He walked in on his wife while she was packing.

She told him that she had decided to go on a trip. Instead, she left the country with their two children and moved back to Texas. Because no custody case or order had been filed, the mother could take her kids wherever she wanted. The dad had to file a suit in federal court to try to get his kids returned to their country.

It became similar to a suit between two countries. The parents eventually entered into an agreement where the mother would have custody of the kids, and he took a job in the oil industry in Texas so that he could see them. Whenever he traveled for work overseas, the mom and kids went with him.

They worked things out. As long as things went her way, she was happy, and he could see his kids as much as he wanted. But if for any reason she became unhappy with him, the kids suddenly didn't want to see him. This pattern emerged early in their relationship.

By the time he came to me, the mother had stopped letting him see the kids. We filed a lawsuit to get custody of the children.

Mom had found additional ways to keep the kids from seeing their father. She would move and not tell Dad. She had to be tracked down. She would say she was going to meet him somewhere with the kids but wouldn't show up. I think she became emboldened because she was getting away with it. It's hard to get into the court to deal with some of these issues.

Eventually, we went to a hearing, and Mom brought the children. My client and I stood on the front steps of the courthouse. We looked across the street and saw Mom with the two children, who were seven and ten years old. Their little faces looked so sad. Their shoulders were slouched, and they were slumping forward. They wanted to come over and see Dad but knew if they left their mother's side, something would happen to them. They appeared to want to please Mom so much that they wouldn't leave her side. Seeing the helpless and sheepish expressions on their faces and knowing they wanted to see their dad was one of the most heartbreaking things I have ever seen.

When the dad did get the kids, they would be distraught at first, but after being away from their mother for a little while, they were fine. That's a sign that something was not right.

If a court finds the children have been alienated, your attorney needs to go to court with a solution to address the alienation. There are several programs that involve having a therapist assigned to work with the kids to help undo the damage they've been subjected to. They show the children that the alienating parent is okay with their reconnecting with the other parent. The therapist also works with the rejected parent to help undo the damage done to them as well as teach them how to work with their children and their emotions toward them.

Part of the requirement is that the parent doing the alienating has to go without seeing the children for ninety consecutive days. If that person violates the order, such as going to school to see the kids, then the ninety-day clock restarts. The effects of alienation are so dire that it requires a three-month separation to try to get back to level footing. During this separation period, the children learn to identify the behaviors that resulted in the alienation.

These programs have been hugely successful. By the end of their time in the program, the rejected parent and the children are reconnected. After that, it's just a matter of how to build a healthy relationship between the kids and the parent who did the alienating.

Parental Responsibility

If your child refuses to see the other parent, you have a responsibility to make sure that child sees them until you get an order that says otherwise. Just as you wouldn't allow your child to decide not to get their immunization shots, you can't allow your child to shun the other parent. You would hold your child down if needed to get those shots, and that's the length the court expects you to take when it comes to visitation.

Children have to learn that sometimes they must do things they don't want to do. Some children don't want to visit the parent. I've had parents tell me, "I can't pick them up and put them in the car and make them go to the parent's house."

Oh, yes, you can.

What if your children said they didn't want to go to school? What if your child needed a tonsillectomy and said, "I refuse to let the doctor treat me." You would say, "I'm sorry. You don't get to make that choice."

How do you make your child do anything, especially when they don't want to do it? By imposing consequences, the same kind of consequences you would use if they refused to go to school.

When children say, "I'm not going to go to Dad's," instead of saying, "Oh, I understand. It's too scary at Dad's new house in a nice neighborhood," that parent should say, "I'm sorry. I know you don't want to go, and this is all new and upsetting. But it's time to visit Dad. You have to have your time with Dad too. That's important."

If you're not communicating that to the children or if you feel powerless when your young children don't want to visit the other parent, how will you make them do anything else?

Even if the child has a poor relationship with the other parent, even if the other parent agrees they're not a great parent, even if your child doesn't have fun with the other parent, or even if they don't like the new stepmom, you can't keep them from visitation. I've seen that backfire. It's a serious enough problem that a court will consider removing the children from the withholding parent and switch custody or limit their access to the child.

Be very careful if you feel strongly about your children not having visitation with the other parent. If you're in that position, I urge you to consult with a lawyer about that desire and get good advice about what you can do to help your children if they're in distress. Watching your child go somewhere against their wishes can be difficult; the child might cry and cling to you and throw a fit to stay with you. Unless there is some danger to their safety, you have to pick them up, put them in the car, buckle them in, shut the car door, stand back, and watch them drive off crying and screaming.

When children protest over being with the other parent, they usually settle down as soon as they spend a few minutes in the car with him or her. They pick up the normal relationship, and their anxiety or hate subsides.

What Alienated Parents Shouldn't Do

In parental-alienation cases, many parents want to defend themselves to the child when their kids say hateful things to them, but it doesn't help the situation. Unfortunately, some parents even consider giving up.

The son of one of my clients wrote a note to him, and it was awful. I told my client, "This isn't the way a little kid talks. This is him repeating what Mom said. He's doing this for her. He doesn't mean these things, and you have to believe me on that."

Sometimes a therapist or an expert in childhood development has to explain to the hurt parent why the child's words don't make sense. The child just knows what they've been told. They can't understand the parent's defense.

In another case, one of the children said, "I don't want to go to Dad's house because the neighborhood's not safe." They lived in one of the safest neighborhoods in town. The children didn't come up with that reason; that seed was planted in them. Perhaps they were told, "You're not safe when you're over there."

With this latter case, we obtained the records of the children's therapist. He read the notes of what the children told the therapist and saw that they were absolute lies. These children would say,

"We're miserable at Dad's house, and we don't have any fun at all. We just hate it when we're there."

Yet, the dad had videos of them cuddling up next to him while he read a book. He had a video of them playing in the backyard, obviously having a good time. The kids were laughing and enjoying themselves. The dad also had a sweet note that they wrote to him while they were with him. It said, "Dad, we had such a great time. We can't wait to see you again." That contradicted what they told the therapists, which was "We stayed in our room the whole time, and we didn't like it while we were there."

His inclination was to confront his children, but that would have made them feel ashamed. What I tell a parent in that situation is, "Your child has been told these things by a person who's poisoning their mind. You now have gone in and made them feel ashamed of what they have done, and that only makes it worse."

When One Parent Changes Due to Illness

Sometimes, alienation can occur in circumstances beyond anyone's control. While my client was hospitalized for over a year, the youngest child turned two. The young children were separated from that parent for that year, and therefore, their bond was disrupted. It became easier for the other parent to have someone else come in and fill the void of the hospitalized parent rather than do the hard work of helping the children remain attached to them.

The other parent couldn't accept that the sick parent was healing and improving. The stepparent had become super involved in the children's lives while the sick parent was in the hospital and had become like another parent figure to them.

The children acted out when they were with the sick parent; they rejected them, partly because they looked so different. How were they supposed to cope with that?

After the sick parent was released from the hospital, the well parent said, "They don't like being at that parent's house."

They didn't like being at that parent's because they remembered the way that parent used to be. They needed help coping with the fact that their parent had changed. The problem wasn't that the parent couldn't take care of the children.

The court considered the fact that my client had lost the ability to speak. By the time of the hearing, my client could say some words but couldn't speak a sentence. As a result, the guardian ad litem was against my client having custody of their children. She said, "What if their son gets bullied at school, and he wants to come home and talk to this parent about it?"

I said, "They can still hear. They still understand. They can still offer sympathy. They just can't have a full-blown conversation about it. These children need to adapt to this parent. My client loves their children, but they can't say, 'I'm sorry you were bullied today.' They can maybe say, 'Sorry' or 'Sad.'"

Then the other parent said, "They can't really parent. They're not a fully functioning parent, so therefore they shouldn't have the children."

It's a sad story, but it turned out well. It has now been five years since my client got sick, and they now have more time with their children, but not equal time. My client is in counseling with their children to help repair that disrupted attachment. That was key. Imagine how awful being away from your children would be, and all you could think about was them. Imagine your two- or three-year-old not giving you a hug because he or she was frightened of you.

Children Need Both Parents

I don't believe anybody alienates their children deliberately. I think at some level, these parents believe that what they're doing is best, and they don't understand how harmful or detrimental their words or behaviors are to their child.

They have the best of intentions, but in trying to protect their child, they cause him or her harm. You may think your husband is a horrible alcoholic, and your children are better off without him. Maybe that's true to some degree, but they still need their father. Children love their parents regardless of their weaknesses.

Interfering with the bond and connection between a parent and child causes damage. Children who grow up without their other parent, whether it's through divorce or the parent disappears or dies or has been removed from their life because of problems—they will be affected by that separation.

Fortunately, everyone from attorneys to judges are becoming more educated about parental alienation. It's no longer considered some made-up mental health issue. Parental alienation awareness is similar to domestic violence awareness. Not only is more information available on parental alienation, but a lot more help is available for serious cases.

Chapter Nineteen

DEALING WITH SERIOUS VISITATION VIOLATIONS

Custody orders are made with the welfare of the children in mind. However, when the orders aren't followed, when the children are being alienated from the other parent, the consequences can be serious.

Habeas Corpus

One of the earliest signs of alienation is when orders are in place for visitation, and the parent isn't following them. He or she gives excuses like, "The children didn't want to go"; "They're suddenly sick"; "Can I switch this weekend?"; "It's too hard for the kids"; or "The kids get there, and they start screaming and crying that they want to come back."

When a parent is unlawfully keeping their children from the other, the court can order the detaining parent to return the children through a writ of habeas corpus, which literally means "bring us the body." Filing a writ of habeas corpus is a tactic I recommend to parents whose children refuse to go on visitation with them.

I tell the court, "We have an enforceable order. The children are supposed to be with this parent today. Please order the other parent to surrender the children."

It also can extend to phone calls. If there's an order, and the children are visiting the other parent, they're supposed to have phone calls with you. The other parent might say, "The kids don't want to talk to you right now"; "They're taking a nap"; "They're taking a bath"; "They're eating dinner"; "Why are you interfering with their time? They want to play with their friends right now"; or "My cell phone died."

As the non-favored parent, you have to say, "The time we have to talk is from 6:00 until 6:30. They'll have to take their bath later." It's very hard; you just have to be consistent with that over and over again because that's one way to make progress.

I tell my clients going through parental alienation that it works. A parent engaged in alienation is going to alienate those children unless you get specific orders addressing it or the children get into counseling.

When I start seeing signs of alienation, I try to address the problem right away and establish specific boundaries. It takes diligent drafting by the lawyers to establish the parameters that are needed, and some people are slippery. If my client is having trouble getting phone calls, I put in writing, "The parent gets to talk with the children on Monday and Wednesday from 6:00 to 6:30 in a room without the other parent present." That way, there's no question of when the phone calls are supposed to take place. You and your attorney must do whatever you must so you can have contact with your child.

There's always a way the other parent can interfere. Then you can show a pattern of conduct. When a parent is acting badly, sometimes you have to give them more rope to hang themselves. Just say, "Oh, okay. So, this week I don't get to see the kids again."

Now you're just record-keeping, which is one of the most important things a parent can do. Keep notes on a calendar. It doesn't need to be fancy. Nobody expects you to remember that something happened on a Tuesday in May a year ago. But if you've kept notes on a calendar, you can say, "Oh, look. This is what happened and when."

I tell my clients to send me a summary of their calendar, and then during visitation periods, to send me a summary every weekend. Usually, they reveal patterns that my clients may not see. An incident they dismissed as unimportant could turn out to be crucial.

I had a client, who every time he had visitation with his children, their mother always came up with excuses why they couldn't come. There would always be something. My client thought, *Okay. I'll just miss visitation this weekend, and then I'll have them the next time.*

Then the next time it would be something else. "Oh, my gosh. If they spend the weekend with you, they're going to miss this super-fantastic, most important party ever."

He would offer to take them to the party. The mom would say, "Well, it's with my friends, and I want to go too, so I'm going to take them. Can't they see you next weekend?"

You can probably guess what happened the next weekend. It got to be weekend after weekend after weekend. He eventually looked back and realized how long it had been since he had seen his children.

He enabled the behavior by giving in. He would think, *Okay, they're having a hard time. I'll just take them to dinner, and then they'll go back to their mom's.* Instead, he should have insisted on seeing them. "I know this is an adjustment to the girls, but they'll get used to it soon."

He was trying to do what was right for his kids, but you just don't let another parent say, "We're not going to visit because it's too hard for the kids."

Police Involvement in Custody Cases

If an order has been issued that says the children are supposed to visit the other parent, and they don't, many parents get the police involved. What the police will and won't do in this type of visitation issue varies as much as the personalities of police officers vary and the customs or laws of the area where you live.

In some situations, the police will look at the order and see that the other parent is supposed to have time with the children. They'll stand there until the kids climb into the car. In other situations, the police won't get involved. Doing so would require them to interpret an order. I've had calls from clients when they have either called the police or are in the process of doing so. I've had experiences where the police will do nothing, and I've had experiences where the police are willing to assist.

If you feel like you need to call the police, call them. Listen to your intuition and your reasoning. Sometimes having a police presence is helpful because it allows for a peaceful transition. Keeping the peace is part of a police officer's job. You're not going to get in trouble if you call the police to come assist you, so don't be afraid to call them.

Be careful before walking into a situation where the police have already been called. If law enforcement is at the transition location or if the other parent is calling in law enforcement, the best way to handle the situation is to follow the officer's instructions, even if the officer makes the wrong call, to avoid going to jail. Police officers are human beings. If somebody has already told them a story that casts you in a negative light, they're going to be prepared for the worst. When you show up rattled and upset, you inadvertently fulfill their negative perception. Domestic disputes are some of the most dangerous calls that police answer because the situation can be emotionally explosive and volatile, so the officers go in expecting the worst. Do what you can to remain calm, polite, and peaceful.

My clients usually call me when the police have been involved during an unpleasant exchange of children. They know I'm available for emergency situations that don't always happen at the most convenient time. Oftentimes I'm able to talk to the officer and give them some background or other information that helps resolve the situation or lets them know what the current orders are. Most officers welcome the opportunity to talk to the lawyer.

Contempt of Court

A parent's noncompliance with visitation can be handled in several different ways. You have to rely on your attorney's judgment about the best steps to take to address the problem.

Sometimes it's enough for your attorney to contact the other lawyer and say, "Hey, your client isn't letting my guy talk to the children. There's always something interfering. Can you fix that?"

The other lawyer may then tell his client, "You need to follow this court order," and the client does. Problem solved.

In some cases, though, the violations occur hand in hand with other conduct and build to the point where they must be addressed. Then you have to go back to court. It's difficult to do that because it involves a great deal of time and stress, and it costs money.

That falls under the category of "We know they're violating the order, so we're going to document it. We're going to write to the other lawyer, and we're going to use that at a final hearing in this case to try to convince a judge to do things differently." It could be helpful in switching who's going to have the primary care of the children if you see enough problems from the other parent.

In the meantime, we can file for relief from the court. Then, if the judge finds a parent in contempt of court for violating a court order, that parent can go to jail. I'm usually not going to ask that another parent be jailed because it's pretty dramatic, and it's bad for the kids.

The judge can enforce the order in other ways as well, such as fining or removing privileges from the parent. Removing privileges, like fining the parent or reducing their time with their children, can be very effective, especially in a high-conflict case.

Chapter Twenty

ABDUCTION AND RELOCATION

When a parent files for divorce or a pleading affecting their children, some courts automatically put in place an order that says the parent is not to remove the children from the court's jurisdiction. That protects everyone. If Mom files for divorce, Dad can't take the children and run off to another country.

Sometimes, this order can be interpreted to the extreme. I've had lawyers tell me, "My client doesn't agree that your client gets to take the kids to Disneyland for spring break."

That's ridiculous, so I respond, "File a lawsuit, and try to stop us."

The intention of that order is to stop a parent from relocating to a different city, state, or country with the children. That way, if a parent goes to Bulgaria, and that relocation order is in place, I can go to federal court and say, "I have this order that's in place. Order the parent to return the child."

Relocation Orders

When people come to see me, I want to know if there's any hint that the other parent is thinking about relocating. I tell them, "Usually when you file for divorce is up to you. But now I would say you must file for divorce, or she's going to move with the kids. Then it will be more difficult to have her come back with them. You can't delay."

The fact is that if no orders are in place regarding relocation, either parent has the right to take that child anywhere in the world without the other parent's permission. If you're married and you decide to go to South America, you can pack up and take your child to South America. If no orders are in place, getting the child back can be a lengthy process.

I had a case once where Mom wanted to return to the country where both parents originated, but Dad wanted to stay here. Where are the kids going to live? Is Mom going to be able to move to another country? I don't think so. Thank goodness this was brought to the court's attention before the Mom left this country with the children.

Relocation to Another State of Country

The topic of relocation rubs up against our right to move about the country freely and to live where we choose. When custody is involved, however, a parent can't just pick up and go; they have to ask the court's permission to move away from where the children currently reside, someplace farther than your town.

The court looks at multiple factors when determining whether this mom, who has been offered this fabulous job at a prestigious university, should be able to move with the children away from Dad. How does the court respond to these requests? On one hand, it would be a better lifestyle for the children, and the mother would have this wonderful job; on the other hand, they would be away from their dad in another state.

The court also considers any special needs the child has; the relationship of the parents and their ability to communicate with each other and work together for the child's benefit, the kind of visitation the noncustodial parent would have, the child's age, and many other factors as well.

In Texas, our court has a presumption that "it's in the best interests of children to have a close and contiguous relationship with parents who show the ability to act in their best interest." If my client wants to move to another state, I have to show the reasons that overcome this presumption.

That's a loaded statement. "Close and contiguous" means that you'll be nearby. You can live in Austin, Texas, for example, and it can take you an hour to get from one end of the city to the other. The distance can be really difficult.

Then the envelope gets pushed a little further. What about Houston? That's three hours away. So, if you're living in Austin, and the kids are living in Houston, you can no longer decide that when you get off work, you're going to your kid's soccer practice or midweek soccer game.

Those are really hard cases. I've had people who wanted to live internationally, and I've had people who wanted to move to Houston or Dallas or New York City, and it's difficult. To have visitation, even if it's just one weekend a month, means the kids are getting out of school on Friday and jumping directly on a plane and flying for a couple of hours. How much is the total travel time from when they leave their home or school to get to the airport an hour or two before the flight, fly someplace, and then travel from the airport to the other parent's home?

To do that one weekend a month, even if it's a holiday weekend, is a lot to ask. You can try to make it up to the other parent by giving them a longer period of time with the kids in the summer. What about the parent who has been handling the day-to-day commitments throughout the school year, such as shuttling the kids to and from school and extracurricular activities, helping with homework, and taking them to medical appointments? Of course, they have the weekends, but shouldn't custodial parents also get away from work and go on vacation with their kids? Making those decisions is tough.

Then it comes down to the best interest of the child.

International Abduction and Its Risks

Some parents fear their child will be abducted by the other parent, but it doesn't happen very often. Below is a partial list of several factors to look for that may increase the risks of an international abduction. Keep in mind they don't necessarily mean the child will be abducted, but it's important to recognize them, just in case. It's also imperative to contact an attorney immediately to get a relocation order in place.

- Parents who have previously tried to abduct their children;
- Parents who have threatened to abduct their children;

- Parents with citizenship in another country;
- Parents with family support in another country;
- Closing bank accounts;
- Hiding or destroying documents;
- A parent who applies for a passport for themselves and their children;
- Obtaining school and medical records for the child.

Allegations of Abuse in Abduction Cases

Allegations of abuse against a spouse often go hand-in-hand with abduction cases. The abducting parent will try to justify their fleeing the country with their child for their own and/or their child's safety. Those allegations can be very difficult to defend.

I had one case where a mother, a U.S. citizen, fled with her children from Central America to Texas. She alleged abuse by the father. We were able to provide plenty of evidence to show that the father was an abusive person and also mentally ill. Subsequently, we were able to severely restrict his access to the children.

If you have concerns about the safety of your child in the other parent's care, you have to go to court and address it. You have to get an order and present evidence to a judge.

After the Abduction

If you find yourself in a situation that involves abduction of a child, you need a lawyer with experience in that area. Not every family lawyer or divorce and custody lawyer handles international abduction. Once you find an experienced attorney, he or she will file a writ of habeas corpus in the court of the country where the child has been taken. This legal recourse is an order that the child be removed and returned to their home.

I've handled two types of abduction cases: either a parent is trying to leave the United States and go to another country, or a parent has left a foreign country, and they've abducted a child to come here.

The Hague Convention on the Civil Aspects of International Child Abduction

Early in my career, I had a case where my client's Venezuelan wife had taken their baby to Venezuela, supposedly to visit family. He allowed her to go, but she returned to the United States without the child. Once she arrived, we served her with divorce papers and orders for her to return to the United States with the child, but she didn't obey those orders. Even though we had orders that required the Venezuelan authorities to pick up the child, they ignored the Hague Convention treaty of which they were a member.

The Hague Convention consists of a group of countries, 83 members, that have agreed to follow custody orders in order to prevent or to try to prevent abduction ("HCCH Members," HCCH, July 2, 2018, https://www.hcch.net/en/states/hcch-members). Each participant has agreed to return children who have been kidnapped or abducted to their country.

Not all countries belong to that treaty. If a parent kidnaps his children and goes to Iran, we can't expect that Iranian authorities will return the children, even if they're given an order from the United States. They don't have to recognize it because they're not part of the treaty.

On the other hand, Venezuela does belong to the treaty but still doesn't always follow the orders. They protect their citizens. Unfortunately, that meant my client's child was gone, and he was reluctant to go to Venezuela because of the risks to himself as an American citizen in that country. He thought that if he tried to remove the child, even though he had an order, the Venezuelan authorities might put him in prison.

These abductions can be super scary. My client will probably never see his son again unless his son reaches out to him. Of course, parental alienation often goes hand-in-hand with abduction. Undoubtedly, the mother will raise this child to believe his father was a dangerous person. The child grows up thinking, *I never want to see my dad.* Also, the mother may remarry, and the new husband would become the child's dad.

The abducting parent will probably never be able to return to the United States. They know that if recognized, they could go to jail because kidnapping statutes are crimes. However, for those who do return, most often they'll just lose custody. They're given visitation rights, which can be supervised so the child is never alone with that parent. It depends on how egregious the conduct was.

Having your child abducted can be heartbreaking, but the situation can also end with tremendous success and relief for the parent when the child is returned to them.

SECTION V:

SPECIAL CIRCUMSTANCES

Chapter Twenty-One

CUSTODY BATTLE WITH A JERK OR BULLY

Within many custody cases is a parent who is a jerk or bully, regardless of gender. They refuse to communicate politely with the other parent. They're critical of every decision the other parent makes. They constantly question the other parent's judgment, and they speak poorly about them in front of their children.

Dealing with a jerk or bully starts primarily with communication. But how do you communicate with that other parent?

The Internet offers several methods for good communication. Almost all of them break communication down to be very short, informational, or factual. I tell my clients to be as businesslike as possible and have good communication. Bad communications are my number one exhibit in a trial. They clearly show a parent's state of mind and how they act toward the other parent. If they're sending lengthy, berating emails, I can use those against them because that's not an appropriate way to talk to my client.

At the same time, I remind my clients, "Always remember when you send a text or an email or make a comment on social media, I'm going to have access to all of that, and so will the court." I don't want the other attorney to use my client's words against us.

Email Communication with a Jerk or Bully

There's a lot of work around communication and how to respond, especially if you're dealing with a jerk. I like to be involved in that process with my clients; not only can I help them so their communications reflect positively on them, but I can also help them send communications that serve a purpose.

When sending the other parent an email, keep them businesslike, short and to the point. State the problem with facts, and don't tell the other parent what to do. Without getting emotional, state how their actions made you feel and how you would like for them to deal with issues in the future.

If, for example, they had a big confrontation with the other parent at the soccer game that morning, they can send a brief email: "It's really upsetting the way you talked to me at the soccer game today when you called me this name or that name. I'd like for you not to do that again and particularly not in front of the children."

What's great about sending an email like that is you're documenting what happened. Now the other person is either going to respond and be antagonistic, or they're not going to respond, which can be taken as an acknowledgment of that's the way things happened and/or they don't care how it affected you or the children. In a way, you're baiting them to behave badly again. Your attorney can help you be strategic about how you communicate with the other parent.

Counseling for the Children of a Bully

The other thing about dealing with a jerk is that it impacts the parents' relationship, and that ultimately affects the children. The dysfunctionality in the home can create problems that may affect the custody arrangements. When that happens, we can get the children into counseling.

Otherwise, I will recommend to my clients that they make sure their children see a counselor. Counseling will help them learn coping skills to deal with the bad parent, and it will also give them a safe place to discuss how things are affecting them.

Parallel Parenting

Sometimes when you're parenting with a jerk, the only way to make the situation work is to do what is called "parallel parenting." This is where the children spend one week at Mom's house and one week at Dad's house, and that parent is responsible for everything. It's as if the other parent doesn't even exist. Whichever parent the child is staying with makes all the decisions that need to be made during that time, and the parents never have to interact.

This type of parenting protects the parents from each other, but it's not always good for the children. Many parents worry about that. They don't like how the other parent is aggressive and yells a lot. The best thing to remember in that situation is that the children have limited time with the abusive parent before they come back to you.

Bullies

Jerks can be bullies, but there's a secret about bullies. They don't have anything, but they make you think they do. They try to make the other parent fearful that they have some kind of "gotcha" that's going to allow them to get custody of the children.

I have seen that situation played out many, many times. A grown-up bully is no different from a child bully. That bully just needs one good "smackdown," and then they know there's a limitation on their behavior.

When you're dealing with a bully, you must remember that's what they are. It's just like identifying a rattlesnake. The rattlesnake makes a little sound with its tail. It has a diamond-shaped head and a long body. It's going to coil up and look like it's going to strike you. It may even try to bite you. It's a scary thing.

But many people live with rattlesnakes in their neighborhood. They just learn how to deal with them.

Likewise, a bully is used to intimidating other people and making them feel small and helpless when they aren't. A bully is uniquely talented in making someone feel that way.

I'm not suggesting you stand up to them by yourself, but your lawyer can stand up to the bully when they're representing you. Attorneys can do that because bullies have no power over them.

When I represent a client who has a bully on the other side, I'm confident when I face that person in court. The situation gets interesting when I have that bully on the witness stand and am asking him questions. When he starts acting like a bully in court and tries to intimidate me, his behavior has no impact on me. However, it does have an impact on the judge when he sees how that person behaves.

I've also had bullies attack me in other ways, such as through letters, emails, and other types of threats. It hasn't worked because I'm very serious about how I handle that sort of behavior, particularly if the bully is representing himself. I limit contact to emails only. If he sends me nasty emails, then I have a whole stack to show the judge.

Limit Communication

Good parents have healthy communication with each other, trade information, and give updates about the kids. However, when you're dealing with a bully or jerk, that's not going to happen. Some of them simply can't be corralled. The other parent has to put up a fence that the jerk can't jump over. That includes having absolutely no contact or communication with the bully.

I have had situations where I tell my clients, "Block them on your chat messages. Move their emails to junk. You can communicate with them if there's an emergency related to the children; otherwise, cut out all communication."

He may come back and say he's being alienated from his children because you won't communicate. But you'll have a stack of emails to give the court and say, "I've had no alternative but to stop communicating with this person because they can't communicate appropriately with me. Their communications are abusive, berating, critical, and nasty."

When the child goes to school, make a copy of the information you receive from school that day and make sure it's in their backpack to take to the other parent. Parents should not have to rely on each other to know everything that's going on with their child at school. All that information can be obtained directly from the school. Then, what do you have to communicate about?

You may have to communicate about medical matters, such as the last time your child had medication or a prescription that needs to be dispensed during visitation. That can be communicated in writing, and then you block the communication after that. That way, if the other parent wants to blame you for your child's illness, they can do so in writing.

This is the only kind of communication that needs to happen between you two. Communication about almost any other matter can be eliminated, and sometimes that's necessary.

You may also want to seek counseling for yourself for help on how to set appropriate boundaries and interact with a bully. The other parent may not change their ways, but you can put something in place that protects you.

Chapter Twenty-Two

FAMILY VIOLENCE

Bullying is a form of domestic abuse when it occurs within the family system. The bully usually uses verbal or physical harassment as a way to intimidate, mistreat, and control the other parent. It's not surprising to learn that the abuser in family violence was once a child bully who has now grown up to be an adult bully.

Both the bully and domestic abuser have low self-esteem. When they beat the other parent down (literally and/or metaphorically), it lowers self-worth and esteem. Their vulnerability boosts the abuser/bully's self-worth, even if it's for a little while. Then the act has to occur again, more frequently with the duration longer. It's like a junkie needing that next fix, but this time around, the bully/abuser needs more to superficially satisfy that need for a dose of higher self-esteem.

Whereas a bully doesn't have to be familial, an abuser in domestic violence does. Here, emotions are involved because of the intimate relationship, so the negative behavior increases in intensity, and it can even become lethal.

Abusers have many characteristics in common, regardless of the relationship. For instance, they may be possessive of the other parent, and thus unnecessarily jealous. They may isolate their victims. And no matter what, they are never wrong.

The abuser may never physically hit the other parent, but they get their point across as to who is in power in other physical ways, which also can become psychologically intimidating for the victim. They may throw objects at their head, punch the wall next to them, or break objects in front of them.

If you have experienced domestic violence, communicating this information to your attorney is critical. I had a situation with a mom who was being physically abused, and she didn't tell us. We didn't know her situation was lethal in that she and her children needed protection. The husband ended up killing himself and the children.

Virtually every family lawyer, divorce lawyer, and custody lawyer I know has had a situation involving a client and/or their children being killed. There have been times that we didn't know that violence was involved in the relationship. Now I make it a habit to ask every single client I meet with regarding a divorce or custody case if there's ever been any family violence. I ask if verbal abuse has happened because not only does it tear a person down, it can eventually reach the physical level and oftentimes does. I ask them if there has been any type of physical abuse in the home, such as throwing things and other similar acts. I need to know so I can help them.

People are reluctant, however, to talk about their abuse for several reasons. They're afraid that by disclosing the abuse or violence, they or their children will be harmed, or their children will be taken away. More reasons include shame, confusion from the crazy-making of abuse, that they blame themselves, or that they're in denial. Some don't think anybody will believe them because they're abuser convinced them that was the case.

When my clients don't tell me about these circumstances, I assume the situation is probably even more dangerous than the person realizes.

Protective Orders

When dealing with domestic violence, you need special help, usually in the form of a protective or restraining order. In clear-to-understand language, this order directs the other person, your abuser, not to come near you or communicate with you at any time. The duration of the order can be temporary or permanent. If the abuser violates the protective order and the police are called, that person will be arrested.

Even with this order, the other parent may still have visitation. They may have full rights of visitation; they may have periods where their visitation is suspended until they get treatment; or they may have supervised visitation to protect the children.

Protecting the Children

The non-abusive parent may think, *The other parent is only going to target me with violence.*

The fact is, the other parent will also target anyone around you. If you're not there, the children may not be safe because the abusive parent can now turn his or her anger and aggression toward them.

The children can then be taken away and put in foster care if you don't or can't protect them.

In many cases, the parent is too afraid or hasn't called the police. That's a question the other lawyer is always going to ask. "How many times did you call the police?" The victim more than likely will respond, "I never did." The other attorney will jump on that response and use it for his client's benefit. Quite simply, how bad could it have been if you didn't call the police?

Understand, however, that judges are very familiar with domestic violence. They see a lot of domestic violence cases, and they know the patterns. My clients don't always have evidence. They may never have taken a single picture of any bruise, or they may have never called the police. I have them carefully go through each situation and document it. They don't need to know the exact dates of incidents, such as June 22. "Last summer" would be sufficient. We then describe each repetitive incident and the facts involved and then *show* the court the abuse.

The other person will probably deny your allegations and say, "Everything that person says is a lie." The judge can decide for themself each person's credibility. When you can talk in a factual way about what happened and the attorney can take you through the situation in a step-by-step process, eliciting information from you, you'll be more credible. Your attorney can ascertain certain facts by asking, "How did you feel when that happened? Where were you when that happened? What did you do? How did the situation end? How did the abuser say that to you? What did he say that made you feel so fearful?"

For instance, when people say things like, "I'm going to kill you," they're usually being dramatic; it's a common phrase. We know they don't mean they're literally going to kill you. However, if a spouse says that to you in a family violence case, the attorney's job is to ask specific questions to show the judge why that was a serious comment. You might answer, "He said it to me in a very low voice so no one could hear it, and he looked at me with intensity and deep anger. He was extremely calm and direct when he said it to me."

I had a client whose husband held up a glass and said, "This is what I'm going to do to you." He then proceeded to crush that glass in his hand. That is a powerful way of describing the event.

Sometimes, the abuser doesn't need to say anything to his victim. His actions alone speak volumes. The abuser can sit at the kitchen table and clean his guns, staring at the victim the whole time.

Then it's a matter of the attorney saying, "So what was he doing while he was cleaning his guns? Don't guns need to be cleaned?"

"Yes, but we just had this argument."

"Then what was he doing that concerned you?"

It's about getting the victim to more fully describe that situation. If I told you somebody was cleaning their guns, that doesn't tell you enough information. It's an attorney's job to paint that entire picture.

Recording the Abuse

We now have the ability to record conversations on our phones, but there are limits. For instance, you can't put a recording device in a room and then leave the room and record someone else's conversation. You can't put something on your spouse's phone so it records conversations with their lover. When you record someone having a conversation with another person, you violate their right to privacy. That's illegal wiretapping.

But there are situations when you can record someone if you are a party to that conversation. Every state has its own laws about who needs to know when a conversation is being recorded. Before you record anyone, please talk with your attorney or review the laws to make sure its legal in your state. Some states require that the person being recorded knows they're being recorded, while others allow you to record someone without telling them.

If you can legally record a conversation without the other person knowing, it might be the most powerful evidence presented at your trial. Again, please be certain that it is legal to do so beforehand.

In Texas, we can record without the other person knowing it. I had a client who recorded her husband berating her. She went out to run an errand and came back home fifteen minutes later than what she had told her husband. He screamed in her face, pronouncing each word deliberately, "It's common courtesy to let me know if you're going to be late."

What made that recording compelling was the sounds of the children in the background quietly talking and playing. That communicated to the judge that these children were used to hearing their father speak that way. They weren't upset, begging, "Daddy, stop," or crying. They were used to hearing their father talk that way while they played.

This guy came across as really nice in court. Of course, he wasn't going to admit that was how he treated my client.

I asked my client questions that took advantage of the impact of that recording. "How often did this happen? Is this an example of the worst, or was this a typical occurrence?"

She looked at the judge and described the incident. "This happens all the time. Every week, he talks to me in this manner." The judge believed her, especially because of how quiet the children were. Fortunately, we were able to legally use the recording in trial, even though the other parent didn't know he was being recorded at the time.

Another reason that particular situation worked out well was because I was able to question the dad about it. I asked, "Would you agree with me that you were rageful when you were talking to your wife?"

He wanted to debate the meaning of the word "rage." Instead of talking about his conduct, he tried to turn it into a conversation about whether I had used the proper word to describe the situation, which infuriated the judge.

Suddenly, the judge helped him out by issuing his ruling; he defined the word rage in a way that really captured what the dad had done.

My client felt vindicated; she knew she had been heard and that the judge understood the situation her family was in.

Safety Plans

Safety plans prepare you for the worst-case scenarios. For instance, every time you're on a plane, the flight attendants explain the whole safety plan in case something goes wrong with the aircraft, and you have to get off in a hurry: The oxygen masks may drop down, after which you have to put your mask on before you assist someone else with theirs. Then you look around to see where the closest exit is. Lights are going to lead you to the exit.

As a result, people who fly know what to do when an emergency occurs. A good example is when the plane landed in the Hudson River. It was evacuated in minutes without any loss of life. Most people knew exactly what to do because they had heard that safety plan, some many times.

That's the purpose of a safety plan. It tells you what to do in the event of an emergency; you don't even have to think about it.

When a safety plan for domestic violence is in place, when that person who is not supposed to come near you shows up, you know what to do because you've reviewed the plan. Domestic violence organizations in every city can help you put together a safety plan based on your particular needs.

If you're in a situation involving domestic violence, you can google help in your area or contact one of the following organizations:

- National Domestic Violence Hotline: 1–800–799–7233
- National Coalition Against Domestic Violence (NCADV): 303-839-1852

Chapter Twenty-Three

WHEN YOUR SPOUSE IS AN ADDICT, ALCOHOLIC, OR MENTALLY ILL

In virtually every contested custody case, usually one parent, or sometimes both, are impaired by drug addiction, alcoholism, and/or mental illness.

Drug Abuse

Drug abuse is a huge problem in our society. More recently, I've seen a significant increase in the number of people addicted to prescription medications. They're not taking illegal drugs; they're abusing legal drugs. But how do we find out if they're abusing legal drugs, especially when many addicts are masters at hiding their behavior?

I have a case where we took pictures of hundreds of prescriptions. The pills are in the medicine cabinet. The dad takes all kinds of medication, deciding for himself what to take and when, yet all of them are prescribed. That's his defense. "I'm taking prescribed medications, and I need all of them. I've had this surgery, so I'm taking muscle relaxants. I'm taking oxycodone."

Oxycodone is a potent painkiller. Painkillers are addictive because they provide a temporary high. A person eventually develops a dependency on that medication, so they constantly have to take it, just like alcoholics.

When this happens, what do we do, and how do we show that a person is abusing prescription medication?

First and foremost, it's helpful to have a list of the medications your spouse is taking. You don't have to know what they are or what they treat. I have my clients take pictures of the prescription bottle labels because they provide a great deal of information. I know when the medication was prescribed and who prescribed it. People addicted to prescription medications often have more than one doctor prescribing them.

I also have my clients take pictures of the pills inside the bottles in case they're different from what's on the label. That would be something an addict would do. The pills are oxycodone, but they'll put them in a bottle with a label that says antibiotics because you can't get addicted to or abuse antibiotics.

I look at the labels to see if all of these medications are from the same pharmacy. Oftentimes, a person who's abusing medication will go to multiple pharmacies. I can make a map to see where the nearest pharmacies are to where they live. Why go to the opposite end of town just to pick up another prescription?

Addicts can be really devious, so we look at their credit card statements to see what they're charging. One can go to Target and get prescriptions. So, when reviewing their statements, it's difficult to know if they got a prescription that day or if they just bought some other items at Target.

Sometimes we have to serve subpoenas on pharmacies to get the prescription records. We may ask, "How many oxycodone pills did they have access to this month?" The pharmacist may say, "They had access to ninety pills." Then, if my client looks in the bottle before the month is over and sees that it's empty, we know they went through ninety pills in a significantly shorter period of time than intended. You have to be very methodical about putting that information together.

Next, I look at physician records. People who abuse medication seek out different and ingenious ways of getting medications. They often take too many pills because they run out early, so they may call the doctor's office regularly, saying, "Oh, my gosh. I was traveling out of town, and I forgot my prescription," or "Oh, my gosh. I accidentally spilled my pills on the counter, and they got wet. I need another prescription." The doctor then gives them another prescription.

In one of my cases, the mom was addicted to prescription medications. We looked through her medical records over three or five years and saw that she had a high number of excuses regarding the medication. If the doctor had reviewed the entire record every time, he could have seen that she was abusing these prescriptions. She had to go to the doctor's office to get shots, but she was supposed to go home afterward. She wasn't allowed to drive, but she did, and thus put herself in a situation that was unsafe. Plus, she wasn't supposed to drink alcohol with that medication, but she would go home and drink a bottle of wine. The alcohol impacted the drug's effects.

Disclose Your Prescriptive Medication

If someone is taking prescription medications legitimately and not abusing them, then we want to know if that person is working with a pain-management specialist. That specialist's records should have a list of every single medication the parent is taking. A person struggling with addiction is not going to disclose other medications they're taking, such as sleep medication, ADHD medication, allergy medication, or on occasion, migraine medication.

I had a client who had a seizure disorder, and she was taking very powerful medications, but only one doctor was treating her. That makes it less likely that a person has the opportunity to abuse the medications.

Testing for Addiction

You can build a case of addiction for the judge, but addiction to prescription medications is a lot more difficult to prove than the abuse of illegal drugs, which can show up on a drug test. Nowadays, some prescriptions will also show up. The problem with drug testing is that there are many ways to defeat the tests, so they need to be given randomly.

For instance, I've had people dye their hair to avoid a hair follicle test. I've had people who drank a gallon of water to dilute the urine produced for the drug test. I've had people who brought someone else's urine or synthetic urine to the urinalysis.

How do we prove someone is abusing opioids? We have to present a combination of their behavior, their prescription records, and so forth, so a judge can come to that conclusion. It can be very, very difficult to do that.

Alcohol Addiction

A person addicted to alcohol feels better when they drink, even though it creates a spiral of shame. It begins with, "I'm feeling bad about myself, but I feel better when I take a drink." Then they drink, drink, drink. The next day they think, *Oh, my gosh. This is terrible. I have so many regrets about my drinking.* Then they remember how they felt better with that first drink, and they drink again. They get into chronic drinking. The same thing happens with prescription medications.

However, it's a little bit easier to prove that a parent is an alcoholic than a drug addict. If someone is abusing alcohol, they can be ordered to use a device called a Soberlink, which is a breathing machine that tests the alcohol level in your body and confirms your identity through facial recognition.

A person can also be ordered to have a blood test. The judge can order the parent to go in at ten a.m. to have an EtG (ethyl glucuronide) test for their blood alcohol over a period of time.

Rehab

Many times when dealing with addicts, people want that person to get help. They want the court to order the parent to go to rehab. I believe rehab and recovery from addiction only work when a person chooses it for themselves.

I've stopped asking judges to order people to go to recovery. Even though it may be the best thing for them, the addict needs to make that decision. An addict recovers when they hit bottom. Making them go to rehab before they've reached the bottom doesn't help them recover. I've had parents who've lost everything—their job, their finances, their wealth, their children—and they still don't get help. For some people, having their children taken away from them for a period of time may be the thing that gets them sober.

More often, though, when the parent is abusing drugs (illegal or prescription) or alcohol, it becomes a matter of deciding what the provisions are. What needs to be put in place to protect the children during visitation? It could be an alcohol or drug injunction prohibiting a certain behavior, such as not drinking or using drugs twelve hours before visitation or while the children are in the parent's care.

That sounds great, except that most people who have problems with drugs and alcohol just can't stop. They make promises and have every intention to stop, but then they think, *I'll just have this one glass of wine. What will that hurt?* Then one leads to five, and they've passed out.

Another option is to ask for supervised visitation so someone is always present during the visits to monitor them and make sure the children are safe. If unsupervised visits are granted, make them daytime visits for a short duration. The impaired parent picks up the kids at ten a.m. and returns them at two p.m. The unimpaired parent will be there when the kids are picked up. If the other parent appears drunk, the unimpaired parent doesn't let their children get in the car with that other parent, even if that might be violating an order.

I tell my clients, "I would rather have you make a bad call than put your children in a car with somebody who's been drinking."

Sometimes parents get into a recovery program and they're no longer abusing drugs or alcohol. Still, they have such a long history, we want to make sure the kids are safe. At that point, the judge increases their visitation over time as they show that they're getting better.

In a situation where the other parent has been sober for ten days, some lawyers will be tempted to ask for or agree to a visitation schedule that has stepped up over time. That person starts off with the short visit, and then they upgrade to longer visits. Eventually, they are granted one overnight and then a weekend overnight.

Instead, I want the court to make an order for what is appropriate that day, not what might be appropriate in the future. A person who has ten days of sobriety may have sobered up by the trial just so they could say to the judge, "Look, I've been sober for ten days. Everything's fine." Then they may relapse as soon as the trial is over.

What happens if the judge steps up the visitation, and the unimpaired parent doesn't allow the other parent to have more visitation, even though they've maintained sobriety for six months or even a year? I think it's fair to put that burden on the person who has the impairment than on the other parent. In other words, the unimpaired parent should come to court to say, "I'm not letting you have more time, even though you're sober. I can't constantly monitor whether you're staying sober with the children when I'm not around because I don't live with you anymore."

I'm not in favor of step-up visitation plans. Some judges may order them anyway; others might feel differently about it, but I don't think they're appropriate. I think they put the burden on the wrong person.

Mental Health Issues

In terms of parents with mental health issues, some mental health disorders such as bipolar disorder, depression, and anxiety can be treated with a combination of counseling and medication.

Borderline personality disorder and narcissistic personality disorder can seem to be the same or similar. They share some characteristics, but they are different mental health disorders with specific sets of characteristics.

These disorders are fairly common among women in custody cases. Although I find the topic interesting as a lawyer, the parent who has to deal with the other parent with one of these disorders will have a difficult time.

For instance, someone with a narcissistic personality disorder will be hyper-focused on their own interests. They're unable to focus on their children and their children's needs because everything in their world revolves around them.

I have a client who believes his ex-wife might have borderline personality disorder, and I agree with him. She makes all these claims that she can't back up. She sounds so convincing and truthful when she says to them that we spend a lot of our time not only trying to disprove what she's saying, but also trying to prove our own case.

What I see more is not so much the person's symptoms but how they act in litigation. My clients, whose spouses have borderline personality disorder or narcissistic personality disorder, worry that their case will be he said/she said. I take that possibility and turn it into "Let's document what we're saying." I request all text messages and emails and anything else that could prove the disorder. I want to prevent my clients from telling the court, "She has a narcissistic personality disorder; she's crazy. She lies about everything." I want to let the judge conclude that.

Borderline Personality Disorder (BPD)

Those who suffer from BPD are scared with no stability in any area of their life. Their actions and behaviors negatively affect those close to them, including their children. The following are some of the signs and symptoms of those with BPD. Fortunately, BPD can now be treated with both medication and counseling.

- Fear of abandonment
- Unstable relationships
- Impulsive
- Self-harm/suicidal
- Paranoia
- Chronic feelings of emptiness
- Inappropriate/intense anger

I represented a woman who had a borderline personality disorder. She wasn't getting any therapeutic help. When I initially met her, she seemed fine. The longer I spoke with her, the more I could see her thinking was distorted. She got into these horrible arguments with her children and had a real pressured way of talking. She would try hard to convince you of something you could tell wasn't accurate.

On the other hand, she was involved in fitness competitions, and she was great at that. She could be very disciplined about her eating. Even with all her fitness achievements, she was failing miserably as a parent and was having a difficult time with the dad.

Eventually, the judge interviewed her children in chambers. He determined that she should have limited contact with her children. This decision was heartbreaking for her because she really loved her children and wanted to be a good mom, but she didn't have the capacity to do that.

In a situation like that, sometimes the best thing a judge can do is make sure the children have a good counselor to help them cope with having a mom with distorted thinking and to have limited time with her.

Narcissistic Personality Disorder

Narcissistic Personality Disorder is treated with psychotherapy (talk therapy). Unfortunately, those with this disorder may think everyone has the problem, not them, so they deny themselves help while hurting those around them.

Help, however, is one thing they need for the sake of their children and themselves. The following is a partial list of narcissistic personality disorder symptoms:

- Lacks empathy
- Has an exaggerated sense of self-importance
- Has a sense of entitlement and expects special treatment
- Requires constant, excessive admiration
- Brags or lies about achievements and talents
- Is preoccupied with fantasies about success, power, appearance, intelligence
- Takes advantage of others for their self-serving agenda
- Is jealous

Counseling Records in a Custody Battle

People think their counseling records are private and subject to privileges. Parents need to know that those things may be looked at by the court in custody matters. The judge may want to see if you're abusing medications you're being prescribed and to know what you're discussing in counseling.

If my clients are in counseling, I want them to continue to get the help they need. If they have mental health issues, I don't want them to be afraid to go to a counselor and not take medication that's prescribed to help them. If they have bipolar disorder or an anxiety disorder, I want to know about it, and I want to be able to talk to their counselor.

Many people are afraid that if they're on medication, say for anxiety or depression, the other parent will use that against them. I usually tell people, "The judge wants you to get the help you need. It's good to see a counselor when you're depressed and take the antidepressants that the doctor prescribes for you. Judges know that people sometimes need medication to cope with the stress and anxiety that can be caused by litigation or conflict."

Taking the medication you're prescribed is looked at as something healthy, not as something negative and that somehow you're a lesser parent because you have depression. The good news is that you're getting treated. It would be worse for your children to deal with a parent who is depressed and not getting the help they need.

Sometimes we want the records of the child's therapist. Some states allow these records to be withheld. Efforts can be made to keep a parent from getting these records so a child's therapy is not compromised by a parent knowing what the child discusses in the sessions.

Children of Impaired Parents

If a child is raised by an impaired parent, they sometimes start enabling that parent, such as rejecting the other, healthier parent. They want the enabled parent to be more secure in their attachment to them. On some level, the child knows that their attachment to the rejected parent is strong and will endure...hopefully.

When there's a really unhealthy parent, you may need to get the child into counseling so that they learn how to cope with that type of parent and their behavior.

The Impairment Trifecta

Some parents have a combination of impairments. I have a client who's a mom of a three-year-old and a six-year-old. The husband abuses prescription medications, and the problem has increased over time, as addiction does. He also drinks vodka all the time. So now he's abusing both prescription medications and alcohol.

Certainly, some part of the mother's character is affected by living with a person who's that impaired, but she is still able to make her children a priority. Her concern becomes "How do I put the needs of my children first and negotiate important issues and make decisions together with my spouse, who's antagonistic and impaired and can't put his kids first?"

Then there's what I call "the trifecta" where it's all three; a parent is addicted to drugs, is an alcoholic, and has a serious mental health disorder. That's the setup for a custody case.

Chapter Twenty-Four

CHILDREN WITH SPECIAL NEEDS AND PARENTS WITH DISABILITIES

No longer is a person with a disability considered inferior; in today's society, special needs and disabilities are accepted and treated with respect. Whether you're a parent with a special needs child or a parent with a disability, if you're in the custody process, the court is here to help you and ensure the best interest of your child.

Children with Special Needs

I had a client with three children, and each had special needs. One child had a severe bipolar disorder that sometimes required her to be hospitalized. Another had progressive hearing loss that required many doctor visits and expensive hearing aids. The third had a severe learning disability and needed lots of tutors.

In that situation, great care had to be given in crafting a good visitation schedule and child support. Although some jurisdictions use a formula to determine child support, it can be different if the child has special needs. The dad ended up paying more child support than the guidelines required because three children with special needs incur a lot of costs, and he needed to help shoulder that burden.

Let your lawyer know if you have a child with special needs so those needs can be taken into consideration. Special needs can involve anything from a learning disability to autism to physical handicaps. It could even be that your child has a particularly strong attachment to one parent or the other or is slow to develop for their age. The special needs may not be something that people think of as a disability.

We want to be sure to accommodate those needs and address them. Special needs can have a tremendous impact on what kind of visitation schedule will take place, whether or not the other parent has the capacity to be a good parent for those particular needs, and whether or not there should be financial considerations.

Attorneys are not usually experts in every area that can affect children during their development, so they may want to consult with an expert or review information about that particular need.

Parents with Disabilities

Parents are often concerned if they have a disability, including depression or something more serious. They're worried about the impact their disability might have on their custody case.

The disability should never impact the outcome unless your disability is a drinking problem or something similar. Those are different issues. If you're a parent who has a disability, you should not be discriminated against because of it. In fact, it should be the opposite. A parent with a disability should be commended for the efforts and the accommodations they need in order to parent their children.

I think judges are more enlightened these days about all the varieties of disabilities, and they don't discriminate on that basis. They're aware that parents with disabilities need certain accommodations.

My client, who was hospitalized and lost the ability to speak, needed somebody to attend parent-teacher conferences with her. She needed an assistant to communicate with the teacher for her. That's an accommodation that should be allowed. If you have seizures and have to take strong medication to prevent them, you still get to be a parent. I compared my client who couldn't speak to a parent who was blind or deaf. That parent would be allowed to have accommodations for that disability.

I told the judge that eventually we would have to allow my client to parent. Parents in wheelchairs are in that same situation. We don't take your children away from you simply because you're disabled. Of course, there are some risks to your children, but all parents are at risk. My own child might run out into the street, and I might not be able to stop him. Accidents can happen with or without a disability.

Our rights to parent our children are based on the U.S. Constitution. If those rights are going to be restricted, the court has to have significant reasons to deny a parent the right to parent a child. Parents raise their children in all kinds of ways.

If you have a disability, work with a lawyer to make sure that lawyer understands all the ins and outs of your disability and the required accommodations so that they can help present a strong case for you and make sure you're not discriminated against.

Chapter Twenty-Five

GRANDPARENTS WHO WANT CUSTODY

The right to parent your children is so significant that the Constitution states that no one can disrupt that right unless significant impairment has been done to the children. When that happens, Child Protective Services, the Department of Children & Families, or whatever the child protective agency in your state is called, comes in and investigates abuse allegations. If they find the complaints are substantiated, they and only they are authorized to take your children. Still, they must prove that you're an unfit parent, and that is extremely difficult to do.

What we might consider nonpreferred ways to raise children doesn't always rise to the level of being unfit. For example, a parent could run a bar and keep their child behind the bar while they work. Most of us would think that's not good for the child, but unless it rises to a level of unfit parenting, the parent gets to keep and raise their child.

Some grandparents, however, don't approve of the way their grandchildren are being raised, so they try to take them away from the parents. Many of them have an uphill climb, though, because very strict rules are now in place about removing children from their parents. I have found that even when the grandparents have a much more stable home or are more financially secure than the parents, which is usually the situation, those factors are never enough.

Then there's the situation where parents leave their child with the grandparents for a period of time, maybe to get their act together. I've seen cases where a parent has been in jail, and the grandparents had been taking care of the children. Even under those circumstances, the grandparent ultimately lost the custody case. Just because a parent has been to jail doesn't mean they're unfit. It's based on the circumstances of the case.

To determine if a parent is unfit to have custody of their child, the court will assign a custody evaluator who will consider the following factors:

- Ability to understand and respond to the child's needs
- History of child abuse
- History of domestic violence
- Substance and alcohol abuse
- Mental illness

I represented a grandmother who was actually the primary caregiver for the child. The dad and mom had visitation, partly because Dad was in jail for a long time, and Mom abandoned her daughter by leaving her with her former mother-in-law. My client had the child for a long time.

The grandmother got to the point where she was ready to seek adoption of her grandchild. Mom decided she wanted to get involved with her daughter again right about that time. Although the mom didn't rise to the level of unfit, there were other factors that allowed the child to stay with the grandmother, in part because she had lived with her for so long.

When I'm representing grandparents, I always tell them that even though the parents haven't been involved with the child, if they come back and try to be involved on any level, a court will allow that to happen. Usually, though, that involvement comes with conditions, like staying off drugs and alcohol. Keep in mind that you may remain the primary caregiver, but the parents will be involved in their child's life, even if it's under supervised visitation or limited access.

Chapter Twenty-Six

OVERINVOLVED STEPPARENTS

In the case of my client with a lengthy hospitalization, the husband's new wife was typical of the extreme. The dad had essentially delegated all of his parenting to the stepmom. She took his children to school, worked with their teachers, and so forth.

I believe the stepmom was well-intentioned. She wanted to take good care of these children, but she shared Dad's view that it was better for her to be the parent than for the mother. The stepmother became overinvolved.

The judge set them straight and imposed limitations on the stepmom's parenting. For example, the stepmom is no longer allowed to participate in parent-teacher conferences; only the parents can and should. She can attend school plays, and she should be there; but she is no longer allowed to be on the parenting front lines, involved in such things as taking the children to the doctor.

The judge told the dad, "You're not going to do this anymore. You're not going to get information about your children from the stepmom and then transmit it to the other parent. You're going to be on the front lines now. You need to step up and be the parent and not have somebody else do it for you. Parenting decisions should be made with the other parent, not with the stepparent."

In this case, the judge reduced the role of the stepmother and put her in the place appropriate for stepparents, which is to affectionately care for these children. Dad should be going to parent-teacher conferences with Mom, not Dad with Stepmom and Mom. Some families may have a good situation where all the parents and stepparents work together for the good of the children, which is wonderful and ideal. But in contested custody cases, often I see an overinvolved stepparent who's trying to take over the role that belongs to the other parent.

I know a stepmom who took her stepdaughter to get her first bra. That's an experience that should be left to Mom, not Stepmom. Also, managing the children's social activities or enrolling them in activities is overstepping the appropriate boundary for a stepparent.

Stepparents who overstep their boundaries can and should be addressed. It may be as simple as telling your former spouse that you don't think the stepparent should be present at parent-teacher conferences; those meetings are meant just for the parents. If the other parent doesn't cooperate, and if there are enough instances where the stepparent is overinvolved and could impact your relationship with your child, consult with a lawyer or a counselor and ask for advice. Give the attorney examples so they can help you figure out ways to address it.

I'm a stepparent, and I love my stepchildren very much, but I also know they are not my children. If there is a discipline issue, I let Dad handle it unless the situation requires immediate attention for the children's safety. I let their dad handle communications regarding the children with his ex-wife. It worked out well because not only did I develop a close bond with my stepchildren, but I also had a good relationship with their mother. Even though one of my stepchildren referred to me as "Mom" and the other called me by my first name, we knew who their mother was.

It was gratifying to be in a healthy situation where we could watch a baseball game involving my stepson together. I could be seated next to their mother, and my stepdaughter had one elbow on my knee and one elbow on her mom's knee as she looked up to talk to us. That showed me she was comfortable around both of us at the same time. I think it was because I respect her mother and her role. She was the primary person, along with the dad, to make decisions regarding the children. I kept healthy boundaries with my stepchildren, and likewise, they did with my son.

My stepchildren's mother said it was worth it for me to have a good relationship with her because I was spending time with her children, and I cared for them. It didn't mean we were best friends; we didn't hang out together, but we respected each other's roles.

You want to make sure you have good boundaries with the stepparent and you're not minimizing them or demeaning them to your children. Make sure you're accepting of that new relationship because it is part of your children's life. It relieves their worries when they see it's okay for them to love this other person. You don't want to make them feel bad if they care for their stepparent. Children often grow to love their stepparent, and sometimes they become a very significant person in their life.

A bad relationship between parents and stepparents negatively impacts children. You can do things to make that relationship better through counseling, online research, or reading. Many good books about co-parenting and stepparents have been published. If you're having those types of problems, it's worthwhile to read one or two.

The situation could be that the stepparent is somebody your spouse had an affair with, so you feel hurt and pain that's real and understandable. However, it's your job to cope with those feelings. You may never be friends with that person, but you don't want to send signals to your children that it's wrong for them to care about this other person because they hurt you so badly. That puts an unnecessary and inappropriate burden on your children. You may need additional help; talk to friends, or get the support of a counselor to help you cope with that situation.

Your child may have trouble with the stepparent. If your child comes home from a visit with the other parent and stepparent and they're reporting problems such as they don't like the stepparent or they don't like how the stepparent is acting, the first line of defense should be helping your child cope with this other person's parenting style. You may want to tell your child, "I know you may not like it when she tells you what to do, but she's a grownup. Just like your teachers get to tell you what to do, the other grownups in the house get to tell you what to do."

Your child may be going through an adjustment, or the stepparent may be overstepping boundaries and not being appropriate. Reach out to the other parent and address the concerns. If the other parent is not receptive or doesn't intervene, then you have to take the next step, which might be getting some counseling for your child.

Because it is becoming more common in our society to stepparent, having more tools available to define that role would be great.

Remember: parents have the right to put up boundaries for the stepparents.

SECTION VI:

TIPS FOR ATTORNEYS

Chapter Twenty-Seven

TIPS FOR ATTORNEYS

Most of my twenty-five years as an attorney have been in litigating custody cases. I've experienced the good, the bad, and the ugly of custody litigation, and I don't know if there's a situation I haven't encountered. In this section, I wanted to share a few pointers and tips I've learned along the way so that you can learn from my successes (and mistakes) and experience more victories and fewer mishaps in your career as a family law attorney.

Accepting Clients

An attorney should select their cases very carefully because custody cases are difficult. When I meet with people who want me to represent them, I don't take every case that comes my way.

In my initial consultation with a potential client, I listen for their ability to put their child's needs first. Those are the clients I prefer to represent; they're frustrated because they feel like they're dealing with a person who can't put their child first and can't meet them in the middle.

But if they only talk about everything the other parent does wrong or bad and how they're a victim of the other parent, I'm wary of taking their case. I recommend all attorneys use this approach.

I've developed factors that I consider when deciding whether to take a case. I rank a potential client as an A, B, C, or D. I don't really want to take a C client, and I never want to represent a D client. I try to take all A's and B's. These are factors that work for me.

Addressing Costs

Almost everyone who comes to my office for a custody case underestimates how expensive it's going to be. When I talk about costs, I mention the worst-case scenarios that I've tried and how much they cost. Then I tell them about some of the best-case scenarios. That gives them an approximate range.

Many factors affect the cost of a custody case, including whether we'll be able to get documents informally or whether we'll have to get them through the discovery process; the amount of records to be reviewed; the personality of the other lawyer, how easy or difficult they are to work with, and the amount of control they have over their client; the number of witnesses who may need to be interviewed; and whether or not we'll need to hire experts. I want my clients to have a sense of how much it's going to cost and how many of the factors are out of my immediate control. I also tell my clients that it's important to be good stewards of their money and to watch and review their bills.

Custody cases are expensive and don't have a cost-benefit analysis. For instance, we can argue over the value of a dental practice. When we discover we're half a million dollars apart on the value, we can talk to our clients in terms of the amount of money it's going to take to try that issue. The clients can then decide whether the cost-benefit analysis favors them; is the money spent for an attorney to argue this case worth it? We can't do that in custody cases.

As you evaluate a case, it's important that the client has the resources to pay for your time and expertise. I've had a lot of people come into my office who are in a sympathetic situation. I would love to help them, but they simply can't afford it. I'm not the right person to lend them money; my family isn't their banker.

If they want to hire me but don't have the money, they need to find ways to get it. I've seen people do all kinds of creative things to fund their litigation, like creating a Go Fund Me online page to get friends and families to contribute; liquidating retirement accounts; and borrowing against their home. It's their responsibility, not mine. It's unpleasant when you're in the middle of a custody case and the client runs out of money.

You have to make that tough decision about whether you're going to continue on in the case and not get paid or cut your losses and withdraw. Clearing up that possibility right away is important.

I've also had clients spend a great deal of money at the outset of their case preparing for a temporary orders hearing. I recently had a case where the judge called the lawyers into chambers. He was doing exactly what we wanted, which was to appoint a guardian ad litem to conduct an investigation that would cover some of the areas of concern.

My client wanted to make medical decisions about his child's ADHD medication and have a psychiatrist specializing in ADHD monitor it, not just the pediatrician. The other parent wasn't following the directions and was instead mixing and matching the various medications prescribed for ADHD. The pediatrician wasn't available to testify, so the guardian would speak with the pediatrician and report back to the court. The judge could then make this decision based on the testimony and the evidence at trial because it was a temporary orders hearing.

As it turned out, the guardian recommended doing exactly what we had been asking the judge to do. We also were able to get the judge to agree to have the child tested. This child needed to undergo neuropsychological testing to determine exactly what was going on.

In my view, this was a win. My client got exactly what he wanted, but it required the efforts of a guardian ad litem. Still, he asked me, "I spent all this money, and what did I get?" I responded, "The legal fees in your case have reached over $50,000. That's $50,000 worth of my time." In this particular case, the parties had more than 1,000 email communications with each other over the course of a year. They filled a three-inch binder, and it took a lot of time to read through them, track them, and follow them. One subject was discussed on page ten, and then twenty pages down, that same subject was discussed again. It can be a complex task because I don't just read the messages, I analyze them.

I had a long talk with my client about the time I had put into his case. He wasn't criticizing my work, which happens to lawyers, but he was unhappy with the costs. In the past, I've been sensitive about clients criticizing or challenging my fees. I've since learned that most people just want more information about the fees, and I'm happy to explain those to them. We talk about ways they can save money and be more cost-efficient.

I'm comfortable with what I charge, even when it's huge amounts of money. I don't have a problem saying, "This is what it takes. A lot goes on behind the scenes that you don't see in terms of my staff and what they're doing—preparing notebooks, organizing the file, interviewing witnesses, and other activities that you're not directly involved in." That's why it goes back to the importance of them reviewing and understanding their invoice. It can take a while for a client to absorb it.

Sometimes I write off some of the bill for goodwill, but not a lot, usually about ten to twenty percent. Sometimes, my client is charged for the time I spend standing around with them, waiting at the courthouse. I also take into consideration that I make a fine living for the kind of work I do, so it makes sense to me to write off things when a client asks, or it seems appropriate based on the circumstances.

When I'm working on these cases, I don't want the issue of money to come up between a client and me. I heard a lawyer once say, "If you're not paying me, I can't think about your case and my money at the same time. You need to pay your bill." Although that is rather crass, it's true. I tell my clients, "You have to trust me to do good work and be honest in my report to you as to what I'm doing. I have to trust that you will pay me."

An attorney has little recourse in collecting a fee that somebody doesn't pay. I've had people not pay me large sums of money. I've had people write me a check and then turn around and cancel that check. These actions are called theft of services, but no prosecuting attorney will pursue this kind of case between the lawyer and a client.

Make no mistake. There are people who are fully aware that an attorney doesn't have a lot at their disposal in terms of collecting their fees. Some lawyers will use a collection agency, and some will sue the client. But the problem with suing a client is that in most states when you sue someone for attorney's fees, the respondent has a compulsory counterclaim for a malpractice lawsuit. That's why your malpractice carrier always asks if you've sued any clients for fees because they know it exposes you to a potential lawsuit in return.

I'm not saying there's not a right time to go after a client for fees, but I would consider the repercussions. I would only do that in consultation with a lawyer who is good at defending malpractice lawsuits because I would want to know if it's worth it.

Even if a client owed you $100,000, if they sue you, you're tied up in a lawsuit for four years on a malpractice case. Even if you end up winning and getting your money, was it worth it? Was it worth the anxiety and stress? In my view, the answer is usually no. That's why it's so important to screen people at the outset of a case to make sure they have the ability to fund a child custody case. It's expensive work.

Retainers

Once I've decided to work with a client, I have them pay me a retainer, and I usually set a pretty large retainer, even though I send out invoices every two weeks. A lot can happen quickly in a custody case. I would rather set a high retainer and have a lot sitting in their trust account than constantly have to follow up with a client to pay.

I replenish retainers with what is called evergreen retainers. Every month, my client has to replenish whatever amount came out of their trust account since their last retainer payment. That way the funds are always there to pay their fees.

I think about the most time that I might spend on their case in a couple of weeks, and that's usually where I set the initial retainer.

I also request trial retainers in the Attorney-Client Agreement. I use a formula to always prepare a budget for my clients of what it's going to cost to go to trial. When I'm in trial, the day is about fifteen hours long. I get up early in the morning to go over my notes and review whatever I need to know for that day. I might have to talk with the client or other witnesses or my staff. Then I'm in court for the day, which is usually eight to five. Those days usually become ten-hour days.

Then inevitably after dinner, I spend a couple of hours preparing for the next day. Now my day has increased to a fifteen-hour day. It can add up to even more, but fifteen hours is not unusual. Thirteen hours, ten hours, those are the kind of days I spend when I'm in trial, and I want my clients to be aware of that.

Balancing Cases While in Trial

When I'm in trial, I inform my other clients that I'm in trial. I don't check my emails or call other clients. I'm there for that client. They're paying for my time, and they get all of my attention. I try to minimize my socializing with my colleagues at the courthouse because I'm there on the client's dime, and I want to give them that time.

If another client needs me, I have systems to help when I'm in court. My paralegal responds to emails or gets back to clients to let them know when I'll be able to talk to them. I let them know that I'll do the same when I'm in court for them. Because I try a lot of cases, I'm in court a lot. I have to set that expectation for my clients right away so they know my availability.

If it's something really urgent, I have my clients send me a text, and I address it in the evening. In the meantime, my team can cover it.

However, if I'm in trial with one client, and I have a legitimate emergency with another client in another courtroom, I sometimes have to step away and deal with it. I have to tell the client who's in trial, "I'm sorry, another attorney has set an emergency hearing. I may have to go over there for about an hour. This judge is going to give me a break." Most people understand that. I haven't ever had anybody complain.

Prepare for Trial from the Beginning

Client's Story

Once I start working on a custody case, I have my client prepare a detailed chronology. They can't give me too much information. I can absorb a lot about the client's case like a sponge, and I never know when I'm going to need something.

The benefit of doing a chronology is that I may see patterns that the client doesn't pick up on because they're living their day-to-day life whereas I look at everything from a bird's-eye view. I have a different perspective. I learn a lot about my clients through their chronologies—how they think about things, what's important to them.

I find it easy to organize each case by topic, such as medical decisions, educational decisions, visitation issues, and such. Then I break it down chronologically within those topics.

I then have my client make a list of every single person who could be a potential witness: teachers, pediatricians, counselors, coaches, and friends who've seen them with their children. If I'm representing a father, I have them list a lot of people who can say he's a good dad. In my view, moms don't have to defend their parenting as much as dads do because of the different views we have of moms and dads.

In addition, I ask my client to tell me who the other parent might have testify and what they might say.

Gather Documented Evidence

I also need to gather records, usually through subpoenas. I find it's easier to use subpoenas to get documents, and I get almost everything I ask for. I subpoena records from the pediatrician if that's an issue, records from the child's therapist if that's an issue, pharmacy records, school records, and any other relevant records. They come to me already authenticated and ready to offer as exhibits.

Texts and emails are powerful forms of evidence. Because these days people primarily communicate through text and email, I have a software program where I have my clients download every single text message to or from the other parent. I don't want to go into court and have my client confronted with a text message I've never seen and can't prepare them for.

If I've seen a particularly nasty communication they sent to the other parent, I can prepare them to respond to it in court. They can say something like, "That wasn't a constructive way to deal with the other parent; that was not my best day."

I usually have someone in my office review the emails and text messages and tab the critical ones. If I see lots of problematic communication, I might go through and review more of the communications.

When I'm talking to a witness about a negative email communication or a social media post sent to my client, I like to have that communication laid out on the projector where it's on view for everybody in the courtroom to see. I can then highlight it online or draw a circle around the copy that I'm using.

Organize Documents

When it's time to prepare for trial, I've already told my client about the amount of time I'll spend each day before, during, and after the trial. My team or I put together little notebooks. I break down my notebooks into a main notebook that usually has the pleadings that are at issue and any relevant cases I want to have available for the court. We also have particular documents that must be available for the court when we show up at the hearing.

I have notebooks for witnesses. Within those are the questions I'm going to ask the person. I type up an outline for every witness. I have found it particularly helpful when I have to ask them complex questions. I highlight notes or areas I want to be sure to cover. Some lawyers don't need that, but I like it.

Don't be tied to your outline, though. That's probably one of the biggest mistakes I've seen with opposing counsel; they get so tied to their outline that they miss a good opportunity. They're not really listening to the answers. Organizing information by topic allows me to listen better and take advantage of those opportunities when someone says something unexpected but helpful.

I go through everything to make sure my notes reference what documents I'm going to use. I note in brackets that this is going to be the exhibit under tab three in my trial notebook. I like to put stickers on my exhibits for trial, but I don't number them because I may offer them out of order. Although that's not a problem, it does get confusing for the court's order. That's my system. You may have one that works for you.

Settling Cases

I work hard at settling my cases, even though most people hire me because there's some potential for litigation in theirs. In fact, I prepare as hard for mediation as I do for trial. Clients can compromise in a lot of ways, so I prepare them for that possibility. I like to remind clients that they have a better chance of getting a lot of things on their wish list if they can resolve their cases amicably.

Unlike most litigants at the courthouse who are business partners or in a personal injury lawsuit and never have to see each other again, my client will have a relationship with the other parent beyond litigation. I have a discussion with my clients about guidelines and ways they can compromise to get something else that's really important to them. By taking this approach, if we do settle the case, my clients almost always walk away satisfied. They understood they weren't going to get everything they wanted.

Going to Trial

If we go to trial, I like to use consultants to help me. For example, I'm not a psychologist. Even though I've read many psychological evaluations, I would rather have a psychologist, who's my consultant, review that document and tell me what it says and what they see as the problems. The psychologist can help me prepare my cross-examination of a court-appointed psychologist.

I have worked with private guardians ad litem to review the reports of a court-appointed guardian. I've had private guardians sit in the courtroom and send me notes about what they're hearing in trial to assist in my questioning of witnesses. I have consulted with other doctors and counselors to help me understand medication regimens. I talk to counselors and value their opinions about the issues that affect children. All of these people can help me understand subjects outside of my knowledge and training.

Dealing with Contention

We're involved in contentious work with people or opposing counsel who can be disagreeable, if not worse. I've learned over time not to get caught up in the acrimonious battles that can happen between lawyers when they're fighting hard for their clients. I want to respond, not react. I'll literally have a tiny sticky note on my counsel table to remind me that surprising, unfair things happen in trial and to "Respond, Don't React"; let the judge react. I want to be able to respond to those surprises as well as I can.

From a judge's perspective, what could be worse than watching two people engaged in an ugly argument? It's better for me to explain the circumstances and let the judge get upset about it than it is for me to come in upset about what happened. Even if my anger is justified, or there's been bad behavior by the other side, it's better for me to present it to the court and let the court come to its own conclusions.

By keeping my emotions out of it, the judge has space to react. Of course, I would like them to react and take action.

Take Care of Yourself

My trials can last anywhere from a day to 10 to 15 days, depending on the case. I have learned over the course of my career that this is grueling work. I once heard someone talk about how athletes prepare for a Super Bowl with exercise, nutrition, and rest. I do the same. That means proper nutrition, exercise, and meditation while I'm in trial. Sometimes I have to order out or eat out. Good nutrition and as much rest as I can get keeps me fueled. On the night before I go to trial, I'm not going to get very much sleep. Knowing that ahead of time doesn't cause me anxiety anymore like it did initially. I try to make myself as comfortable as possible and rest, knowing that as soon as the trial is over, I'm going to get more sleep.

Custody cases are hard work, but it's gratifying work. I usually won't meet the children at stake. It helps me keep a proper amount of detachment. I only know about them through pictures and what their parents have said about them.

A lot of people ask me if I lose sleep over my job. The answer is sure, sometimes I do. But I've also learned that it's beneficial for everyone, including myself, to not constantly worry and think about my cases or my clients or their children. I have a job to do for the people, and the more lovingly detached I can be from their situation, the better.

About the Author

JANET McCULLAR

Janet McCullar is one of the top nationally respected divorce and custody trial attorneys, known for her skill, strategy, and success in the courtroom. She has represented clients in hundreds of complex divorce and custody cases. She also uses her seasoned skills outside the courtroom to amicably resolve cases whenever possible to save her clients the time, cost, and pain that's involved in litigation.

Her motivation isn't about the case; it's about her clients. Her passion stems not only from her education in the area of divorce and custody but also as a result of her experience of walking through her own divorce and the challenges it brought. She knows that divorce is never easy; it's a messy situation, but working together with her clients for the best interest of the children is essential to a healthier outcome.

Janet's impressive credentials in the custody and divorce area of practice include being Board Certified in Family Law by the Texas Board of Legal Specialization, and she was also selected to be a Fellow in the prestigious American Academy of Matrimonial Lawyers, an organization of the nation's top divorce attorneys, an honor that comes from their intense vetting process.

The intricacy of walking through the unknowns of the custody process is scary and intimidating. This is why Janet is now offering online coaching at JanetMcCullar.com for those who need quick advice but don't want to yet pay the retainer needed to secure an attorney.

Away from the office, Janet is a mother of three children and a strong Christian who depends very much on her faith. Her other passions include fitness, learning to sail, reading, the arts, traveling, and community service.

To consult with the author, visit https://janetmccullar.com.